VOLUME 14

DELUXE GUITAR PLAY-ALONG

AUDIO ACCESS INCLUDED

T0039446

Cover photo © MediaPunch Inc / Alamy Stock Photo

PLAYBACK+
Speed · Pitch · Balance · Loop

To access audio visit:
www.halleonard.com/mylibrary

Enter Code
2803-8058-9669-7481

ISBN 978-1-5400-4250-7

HAL•LEONARD®

Visit Hal Leonard Online at
www.halleonard.com

Contact us:
Hal Leonard
7777 West Bluemound Road
Milwaukee, WI 53213
Email: info@halleonard.com

In Europe, contact:
Hal Leonard Europe Limited
42 Wigmore Street
Marylebone, London, W1U 2RN
Email: info@halleonardeurope.com

In Australia, contact:
Hal Leonard Australia Pty. Ltd.
4 Lentara Court
Cheltenham, Victoria, 3192 Australia
Email: info@halleonard.com.au

T0071357

GUITAR NOTATION LEGEND

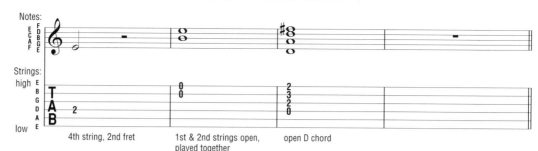

THE MUSICAL STAFF shows pitches and rhythms and is divided by bar lines into measures. Pitches are named after the first seven letters of the alphabet.

TABLATURE graphically represents the guitar fingerboard. Each horizontal line represents a string, and each number represents a fret.

4th string, 2nd fret

1st & 2nd strings open, played together

open D chord

HALF-STEP BEND: Strike the note and bend up 1/2 step.

WHOLE-STEP BEND: Strike the note and bend up one step.

GRACE NOTE BEND: Strike the note and immediately bend up as indicated.

SLIGHT (MICROTONE) BEND: Strike the note and bend up 1/4 step.

BEND AND RELEASE: Strike the note and bend up as indicated, then release back to the original note. Only the first note is struck.

PRE-BEND: Bend the note as indicated, then strike it.

VIBRATO: The string is vibrated by rapidly bending and releasing the note with the fretting hand.

PALM MUTING: The note is partially muted by the pick hand lightly touching the string(s) just before the bridge.

HAMMER-ON: Strike the first (lower) note with one finger, then sound the higher note (on the same string) with another finger by fretting it without picking.

PULL-OFF: Place both fingers on the notes to be sounded. Strike the first note and without picking, pull the finger off to sound the second (lower) note.

LEGATO SLIDE: Strike the first note and then slide the same fret-hand finger up or down to the second note. The second note is not struck.

SHIFT SLIDE: Same as legato slide, except the second note is struck.

TRILL: Very rapidly alternate between the notes indicated by continuously hammering on and pulling off.

TAPPING: Hammer ("tap") the fret indicated with the pick-hand index or middle finger and pull off to the note fretted by the fret hand.

NATURAL HARMONIC: Strike the note while the fret-hand lightly touches the string directly over the fret indicated.

PINCH HARMONIC: The note is fretted normally and a harmonic is produced by adding the edge of the thumb or the tip of the index finger of the pick hand to the normal pick attack.

TREMOLO PICKING: The note is picked as rapidly and continuously as possible.

VIBRATO BAR DIVE AND RETURN: The pitch of the note or chord is dropped a specified number of steps (in rhythm), then returned to the original pitch.

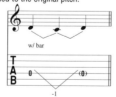

VIBRATO BAR SCOOP: Depress the bar just before striking the note, then quickly release the bar.

VIBRATO BAR DIP: Strike the note and then immediately drop a specified number of steps, then release back to the original pitch.

Additional Musical Definitions

 *(accent)* • Accentuate note (play it louder).

 *(staccato)* • Play the note short.

D.S. al Coda • Go back to the sign (𝄋), then play until the measure marked "*To Coda*," then skip to the section labelled "*Coda*."

D.C. al Fine • Go back to the beginning of the song and play until the measure marked "*Fine*" (end).

Fill • Label used to identify a brief melodic figure which is to be inserted into the arrangement.

N.C. • Harmony is implied.

  • Repeat measures between signs.

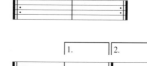 • When a repeated section has different endings, play the first ending only the first time and the second ending only the second time.

Against The Wind

Words and Music by Bob Seger

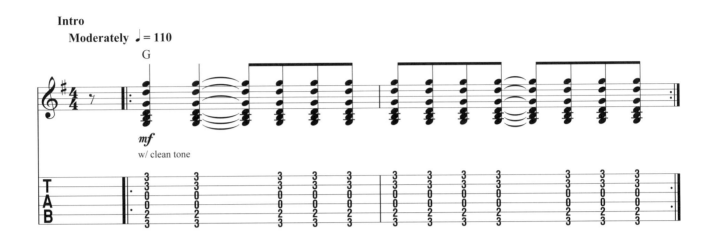

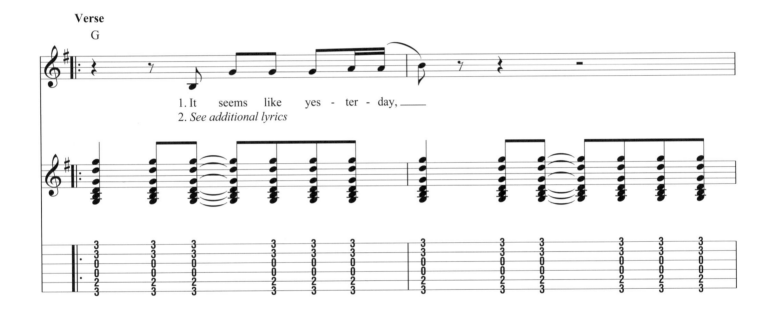

1. It seems like yes - ter - day, ____
2. *See additional lyrics*

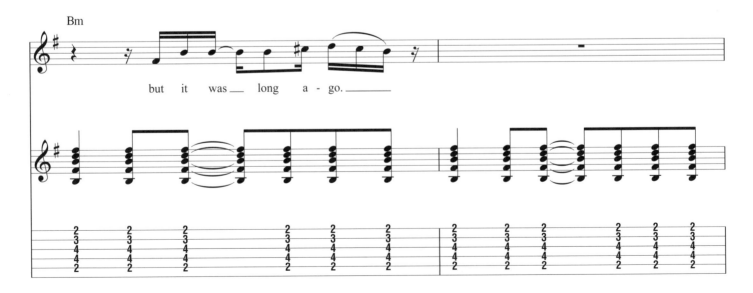

but it was ____ long a - go. ____

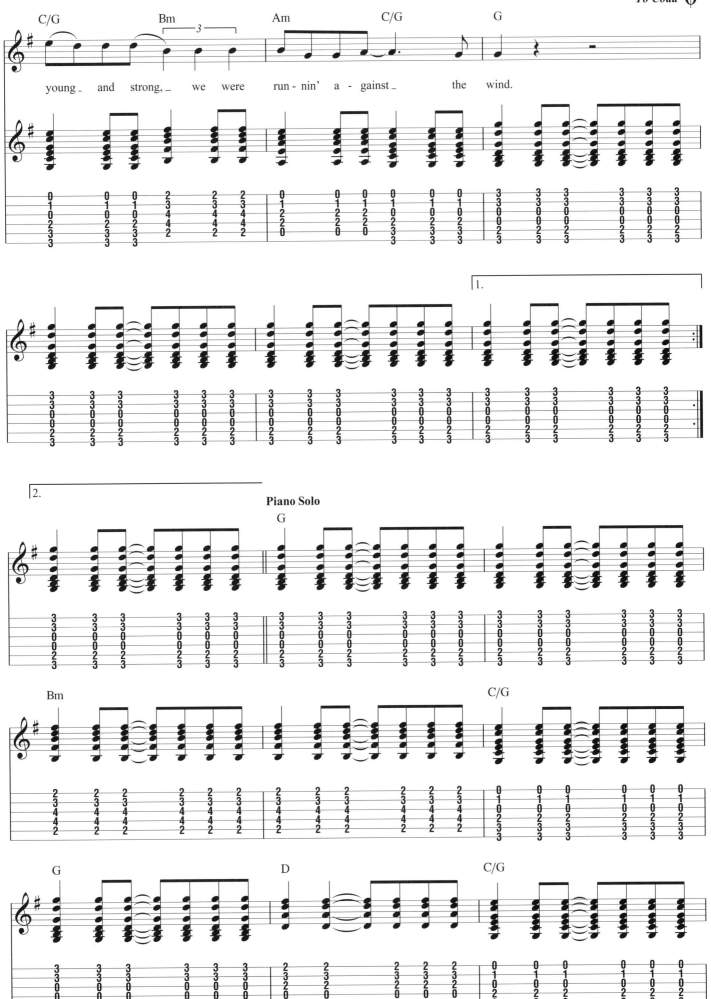

young _ and strong, _ we were run - nin' a - gainst _ the wind.

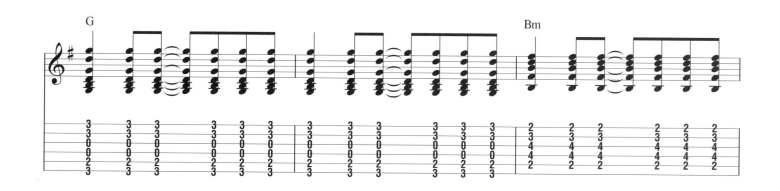

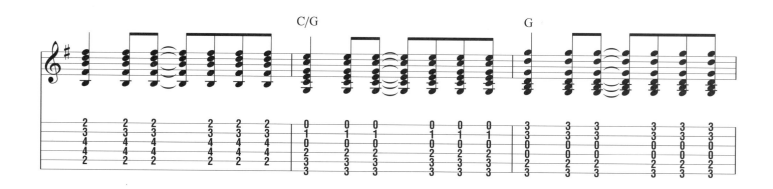

3. Well, those

Well, I'm old - er now ___ and still

Outro

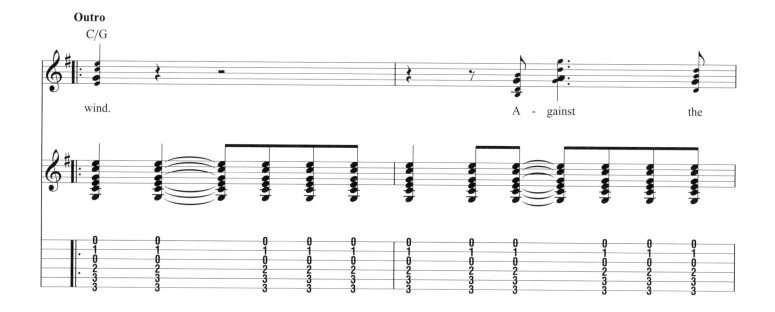

wind.   A - gainst   the

Repeat and fade

wind.   A - gainst   the

Additional Lyrics

2. And the years rolled slowly past,
   And I found myself alone.
   Surrounded by strangers I thought were my friends.
   I found myself further and further from my home.
   And I guess I lost my way.
   There were, oh, so many roads.
   I was living to run and running to live.
   Never worried about paying or even how much I owed.

Pre-Chorus 2. Moving eight miles a minute for months at a time.
   Breaking all of the rules that we bent.
   I began to find myself searching,
   Searching for shelter again and again.

Chorus 2. Against the wind,
   Little something against the wind.
   I found myself seeking shelter against the wind.

Pre-Chorus 3. Well, those drifter's days are past me now.
   I've got so much more to think about.
   Deadlines and commitments,
   What to leave in, what to leave out.

Chorus 3. Against the wind,
   I'm still runnin' against the wind.
   I'm older now but still runnin' against the wind.

Feel Like A Number

Words and Music by Bob Seger

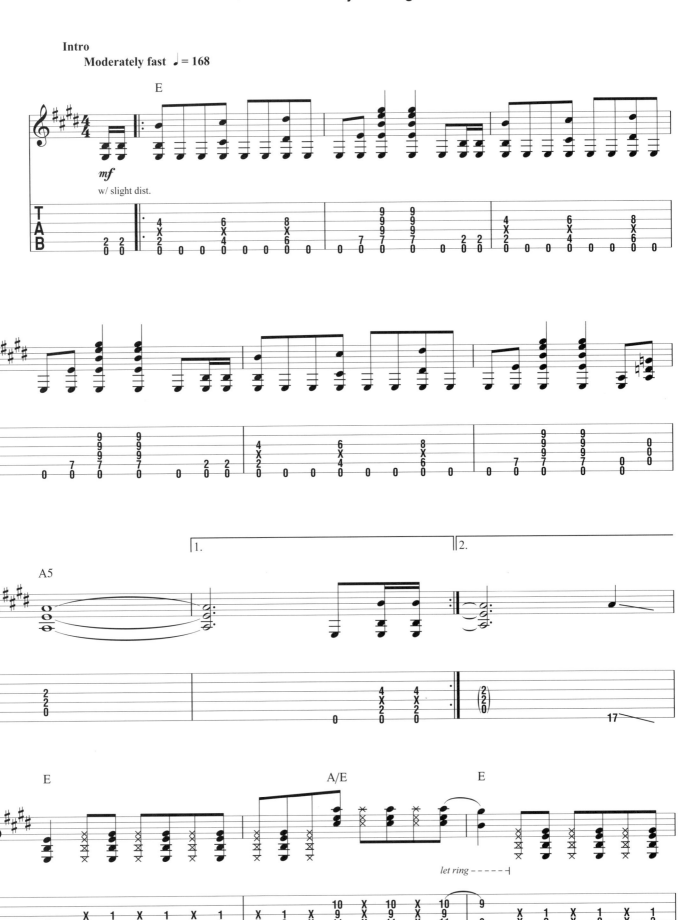

Verse

1. I take my card and I stand in line. To
2. *See additional lyrics*

make a buck, I work o - ver - time. "Dear Sir" let - ters keep com -

- in' in the mail.

work my back 'til it's racked with pain. The boss can't e - ven re - call

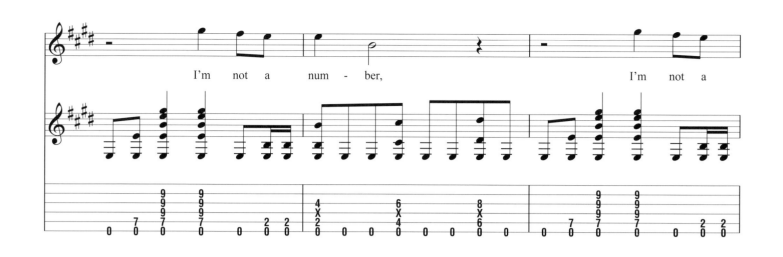

I'm not a num - ber,   I'm not a

To Coda 2 ⊕

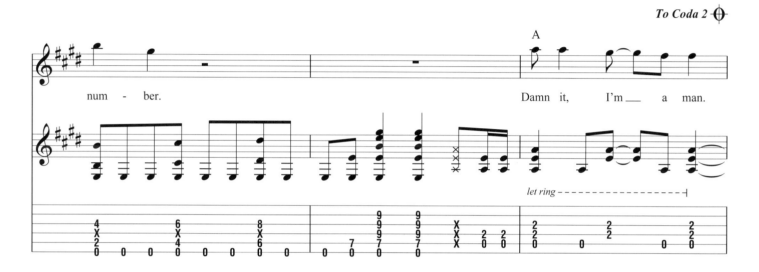

num - ber.   Damn it, I'm___ a man.

let ring -----------------

Piano Solo

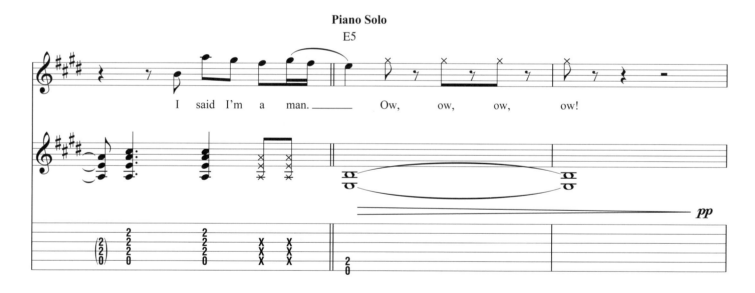

I said I'm a man.___ Ow, ow, ow, ow!

pp

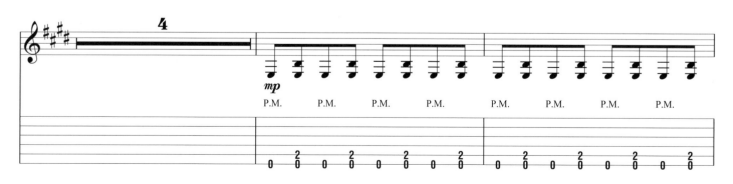

mp

P.M. P.M. P.M. P.M. P.M. P.M. P.M. P.M.

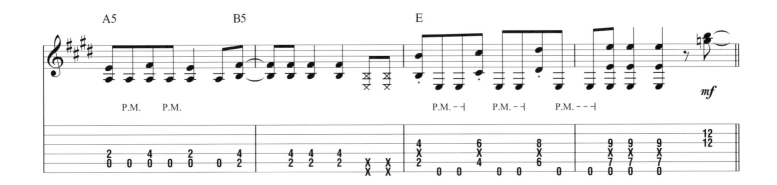

Guitar Solo

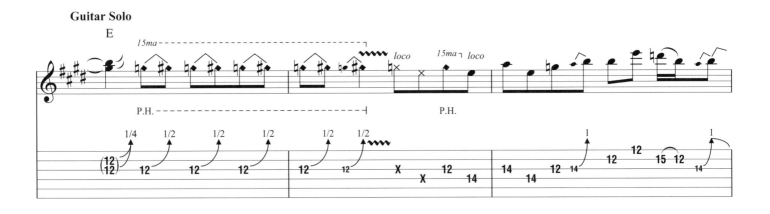

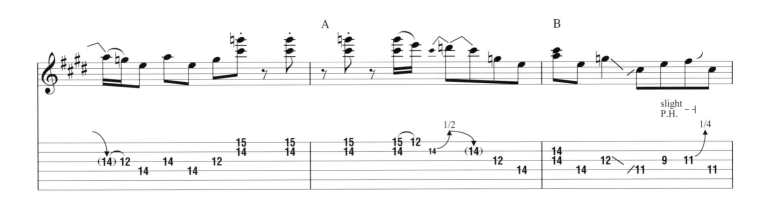

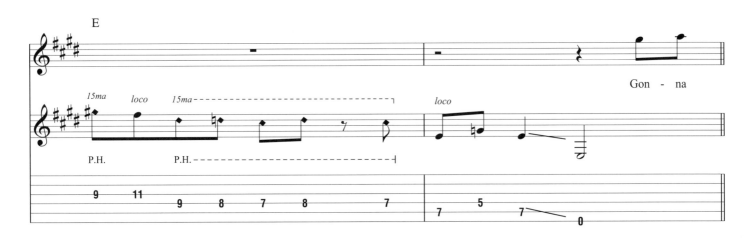

Pre-Chorus

D.S.S. al Coda 2

Coda 2

Outro-Chorus

Additional Lyrics

2. To workers, I'm just another drone.
   To Ma Bell, I'm just another phone.
   I'm just another statistic on a sheet.
   To teachers, I'm just another child.
   To IRS, I'm another file.
   I'm just another consensus on the street.

The Fire Down Below

Words and Music by Bob Seger

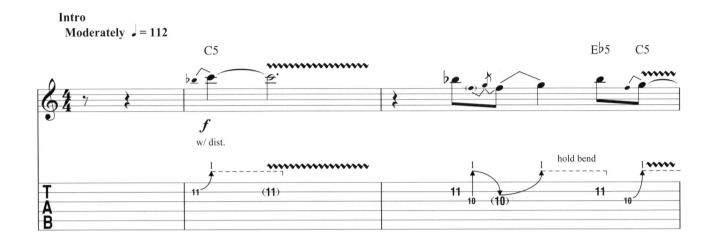

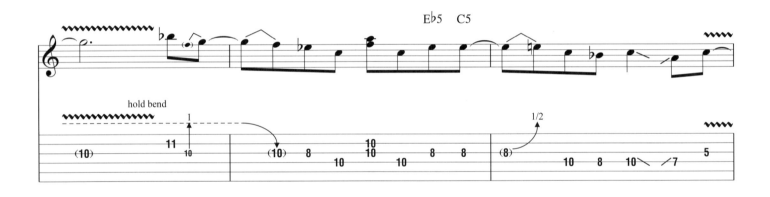

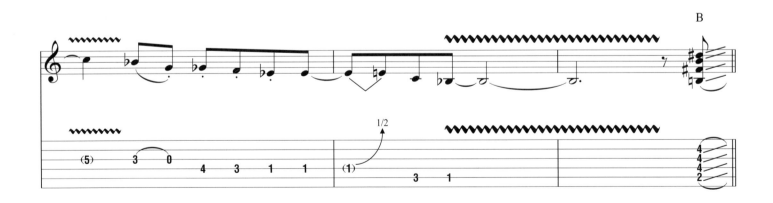

Verse

2nd time, substitute Fill 1

1. Here comes old Ros - ie, she's look - ing might - y fine;
2. *See additional lyrics*

here comes hot Nan - cy, she's step - pin' right on time.

There go the street lights, bring - ing on the night;

Fill 1

here come the men, fac-es hid-den from the light.

F5   **E♭5**

All through the shad-ows,   oh,   they come and they go.

C5

With on - ly one

let ring

G5   **F5**

thing in com-mon,   they got the fire down be-low.

2nd time, substitute Fill 2

go - ing on ___ to - night. ___ Some - where there's some - bod - y ain't treat - in' ___

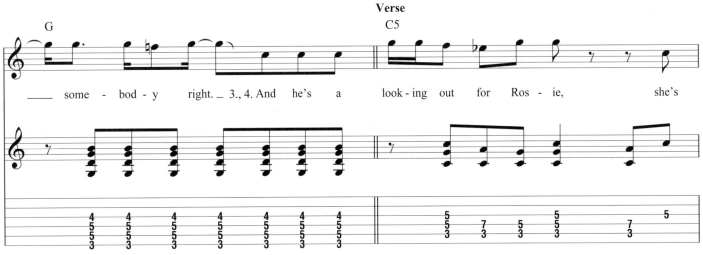

Verse

___ some - bod - y right. ___ 3., 4. And he's a look - ing out for Ros - ie, she's

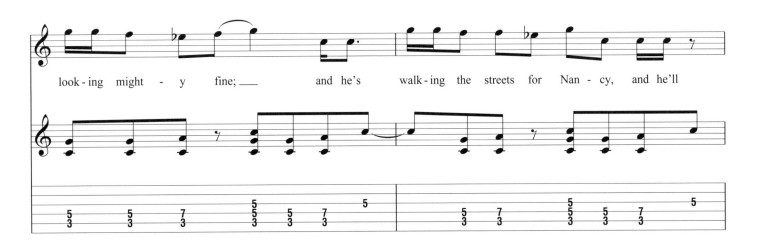

look - ing might - y fine; ___ and he's walk - ing the streets for Nan - cy, and he'll

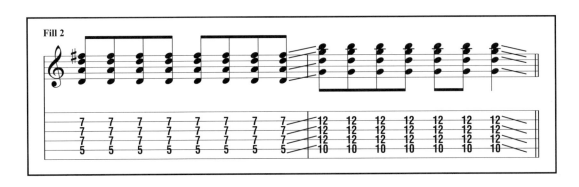

Fill 2

2nd time, substitute Fill 3

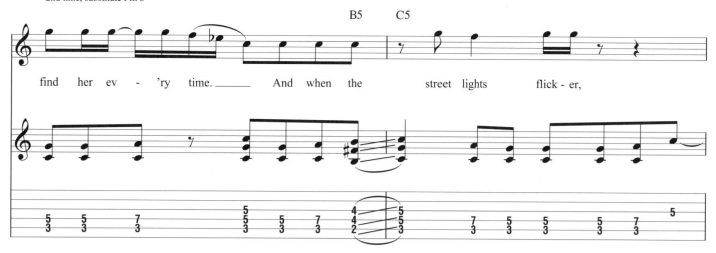

find her ev - 'ry time. _____ And when the street lights flick - er,

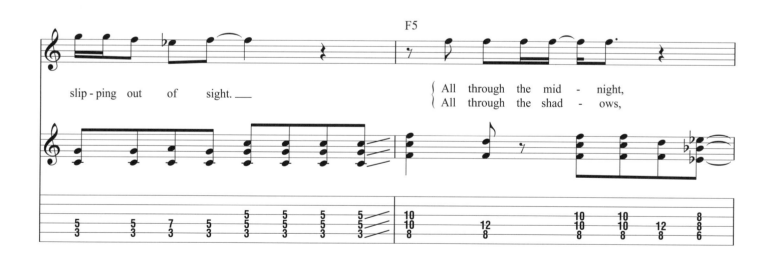

bring - ing on the night, ___ well, they'll be slip - ping in - to dark - ness,

slip - ping out of sight. ___ { All through the mid - night,
{ All through the shad - ows,

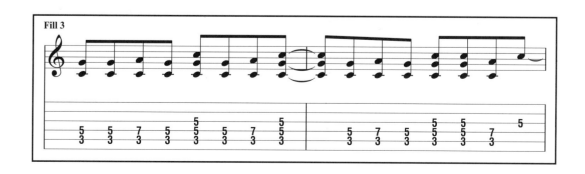

Fill 3

watch 'em come and watch 'em go, _____ oh,
watch 'em come and watch 'em go, _____ oh, they

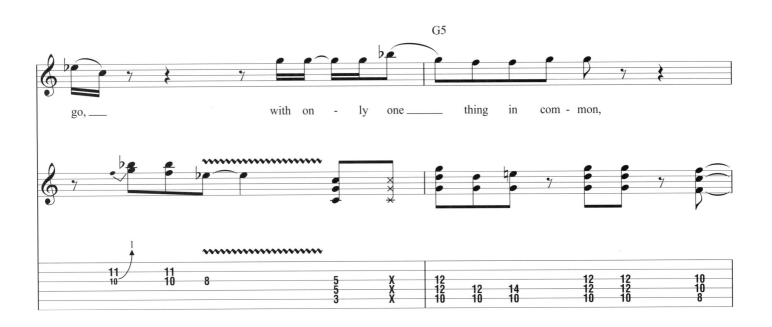

go, _____ with on - ly one _____ thing in com - mon,

To Coda ⊕

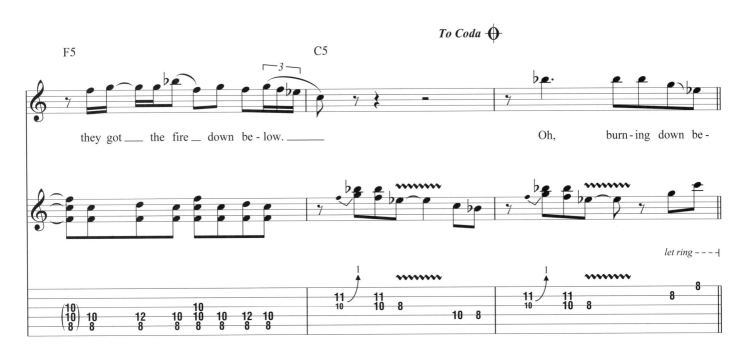

they got _____ the fire _____ down be - low. _____ Oh, burn - ing down be -

let ring - - - -|

Guitar Solo

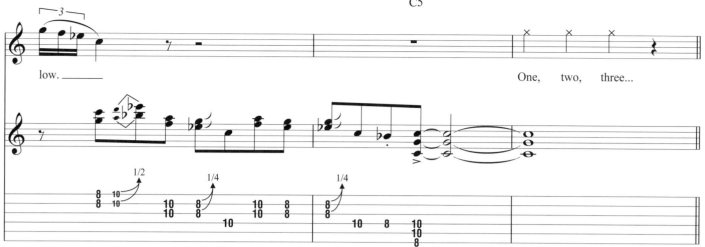

Outro-Guitar Solo

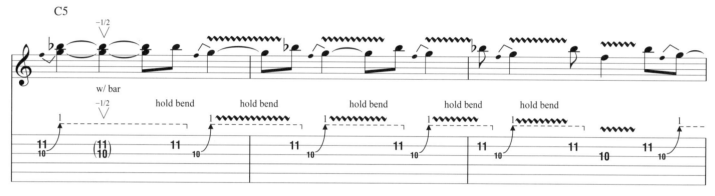

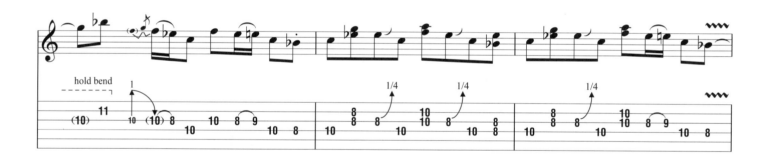

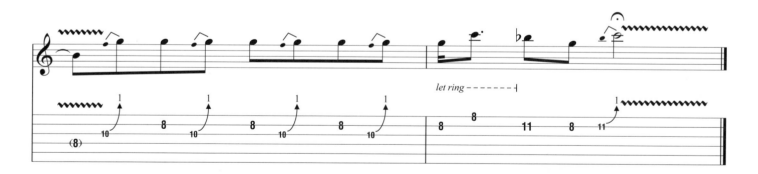

Additional Lyrics

2. Here comes the rich man in his big long limousine;
   Here comes the poor man, all you got to have is green.
   Here comes the banker, and the lawyer and the cop;
   One thing for certain, it ain't never gonna stop.
   When it all gets too heavy, that's when they come and they go, they go.
   With only one thing in common, they got the fire down below.

Fire Lake

Words and Music by Bob Seger

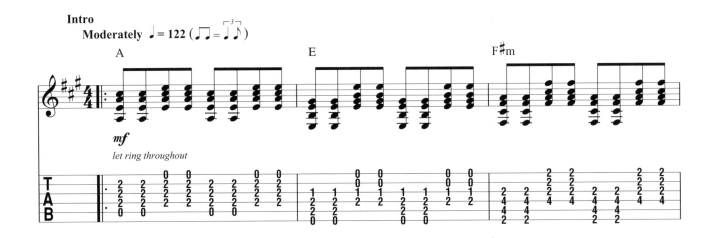

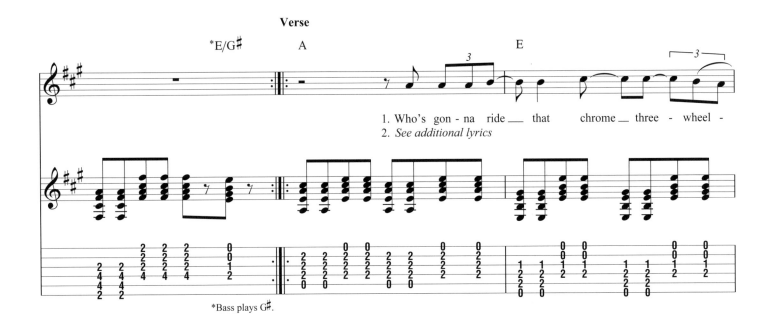

1. Who's gon - na ride __ that chrome __ three - wheel -
2. *See additional lyrics*

*Bass plays G#.

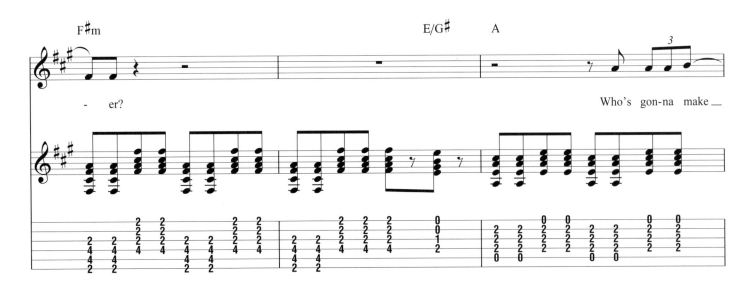

- er?

Who's gon - na make __

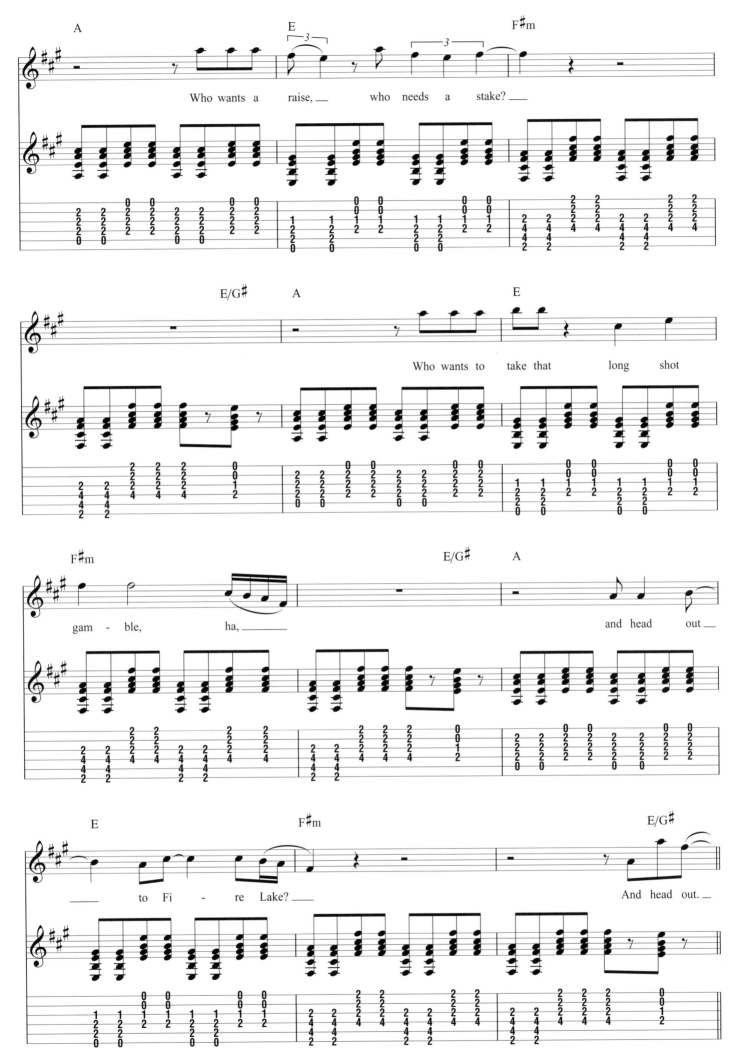

Additional Lyrics

2. Who wants to break the news about Uncle Joe?
   You remember Uncle Joe; he was the one afraid to cut the cake.
   Who wants to tell poor Aunt Sarah,
   Joe has run off to Fire Lake?
   Joe has run off to Fire Lake.

Her Strut

Words and Music by Bob Seger

Tune down 1/2 step:
(low to high) Eb-Ab-Db-Gb-Bb-Eb

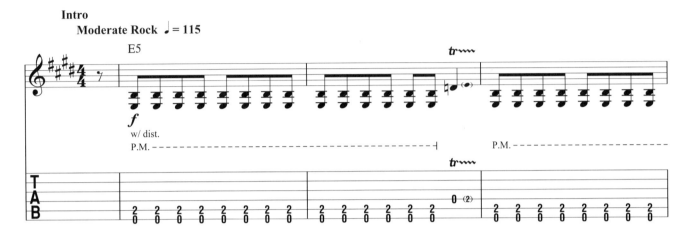

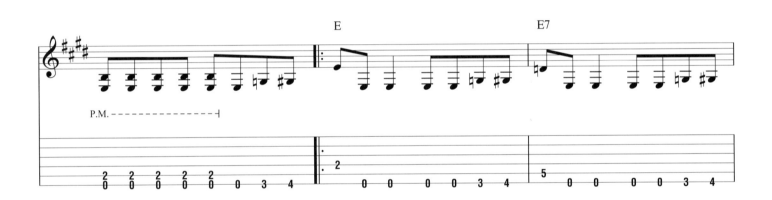

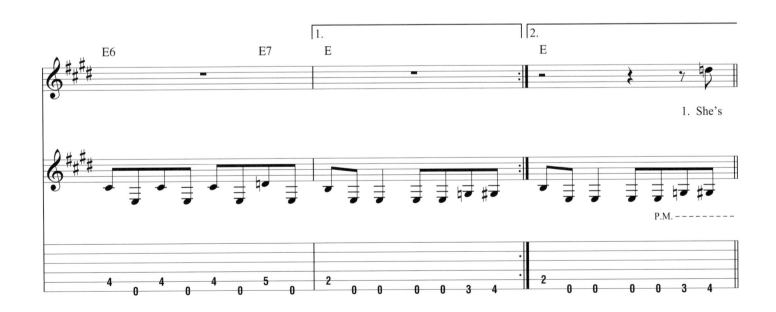

1. She's

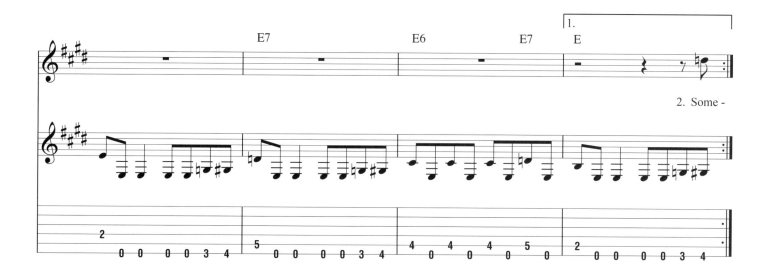

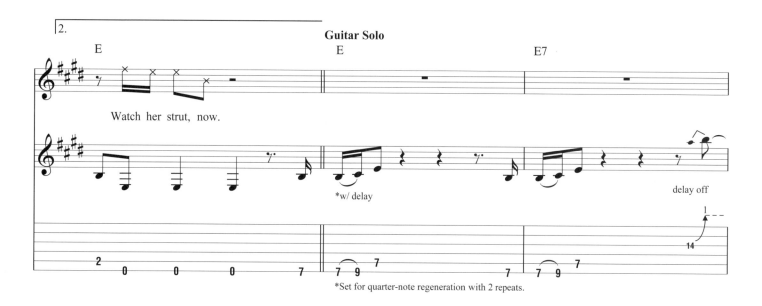

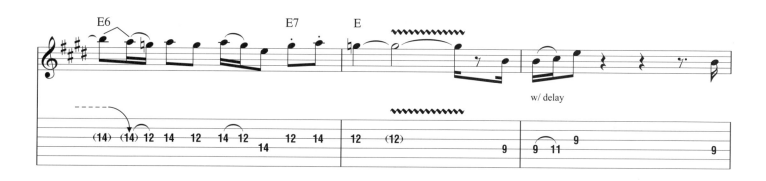

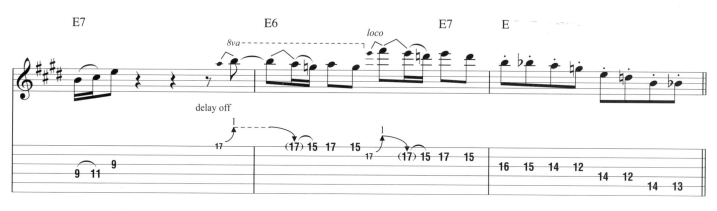

Outro

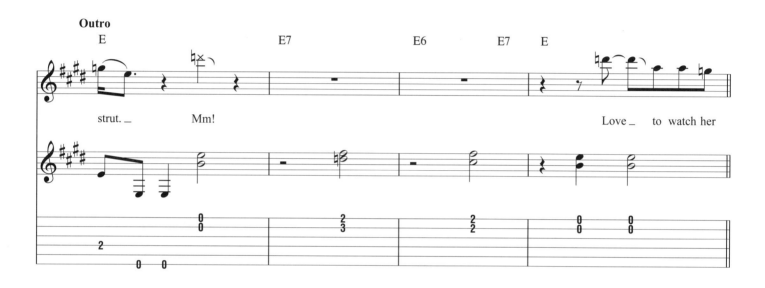

Repeat and fade

w/ Voc. ad lib. on repeats

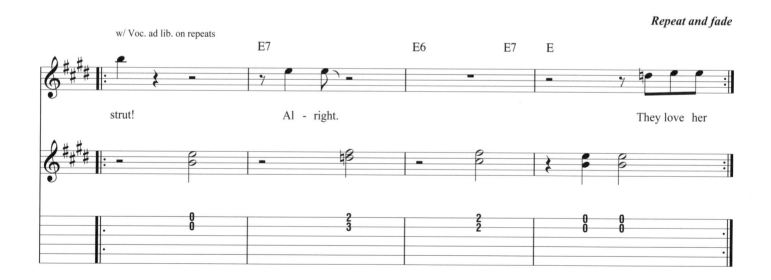

Additional Lyrics

2. Sometimes they'll want to leave her, just give up and leave her,
   But they would never play that scene.
   In spite of all her talking, once she starts in walking,
   The lady will be all they ever dreamed.

Chorus Oh, they'll love to watch her strut.
   Oh, they'll kill to make the cut,
   They love to watch her strut.

Hollywood Nights

Words and Music by Bob Seger

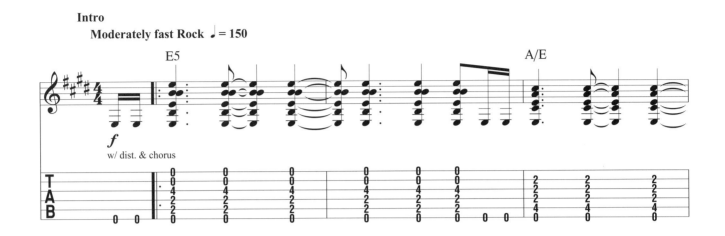

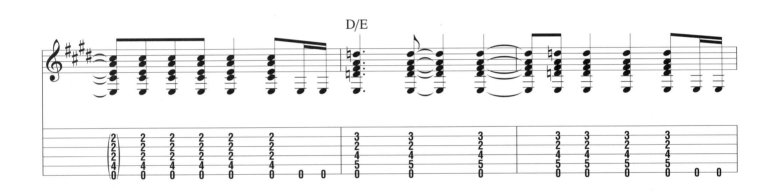

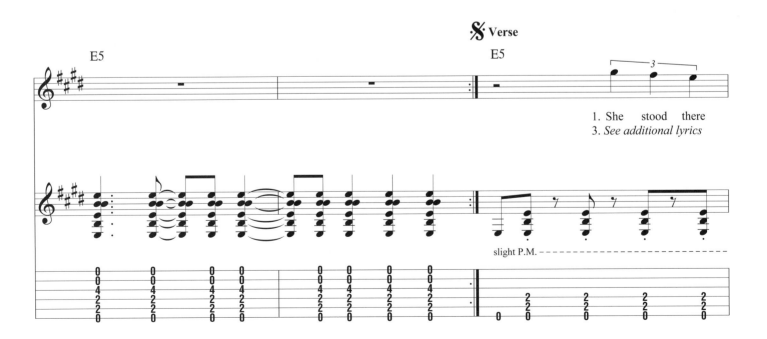

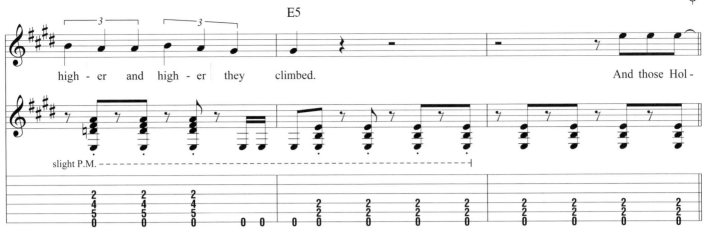

high-er and high-er they climbed.

And those Hol -

slight P.M.

Chorus

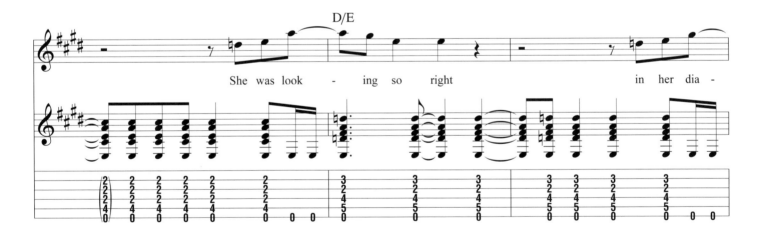

- ly-wood nights

in those Hol - ly-wood hills.

She was look - ing so right

in her dia -

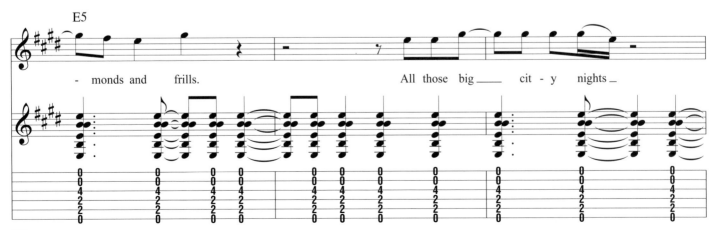

- monds and frills.

All those big___ cit-y nights___

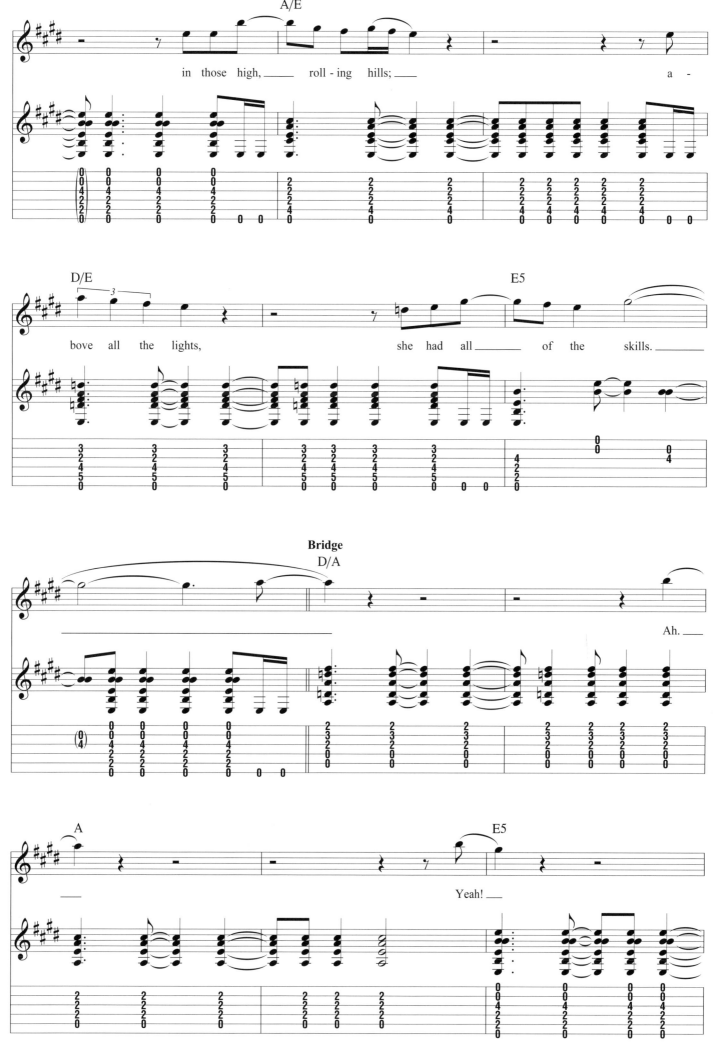

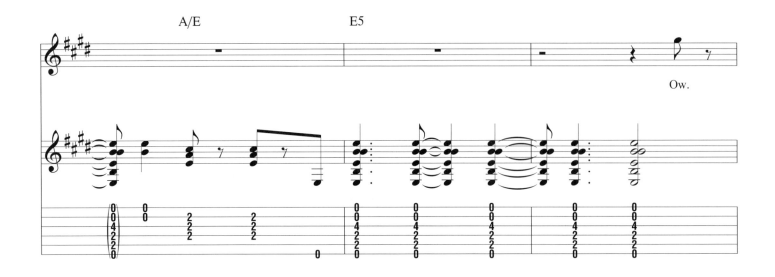

Ow.

D.S. al Coda

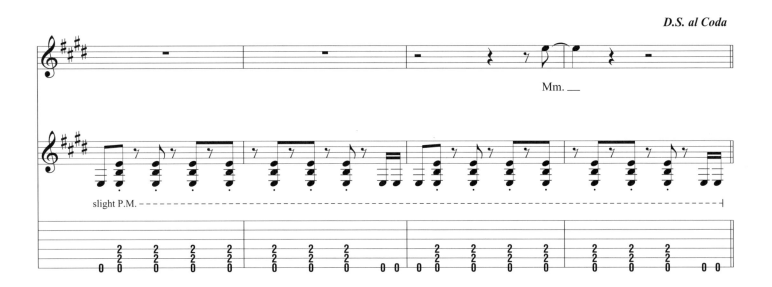

Mm. ___

slight P.M.

Coda

Chorus

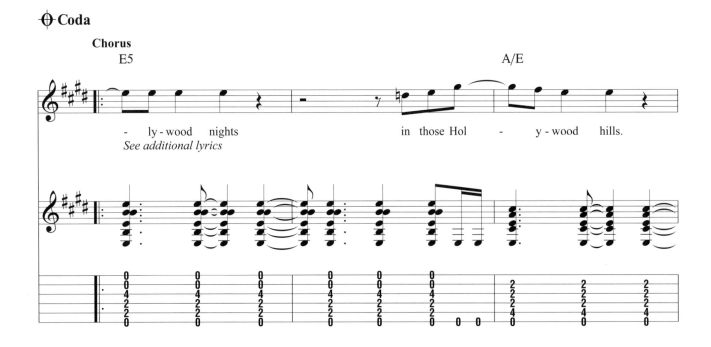

\- ly-wood nights   in those Hol - y - wood hills.
See additional lyrics

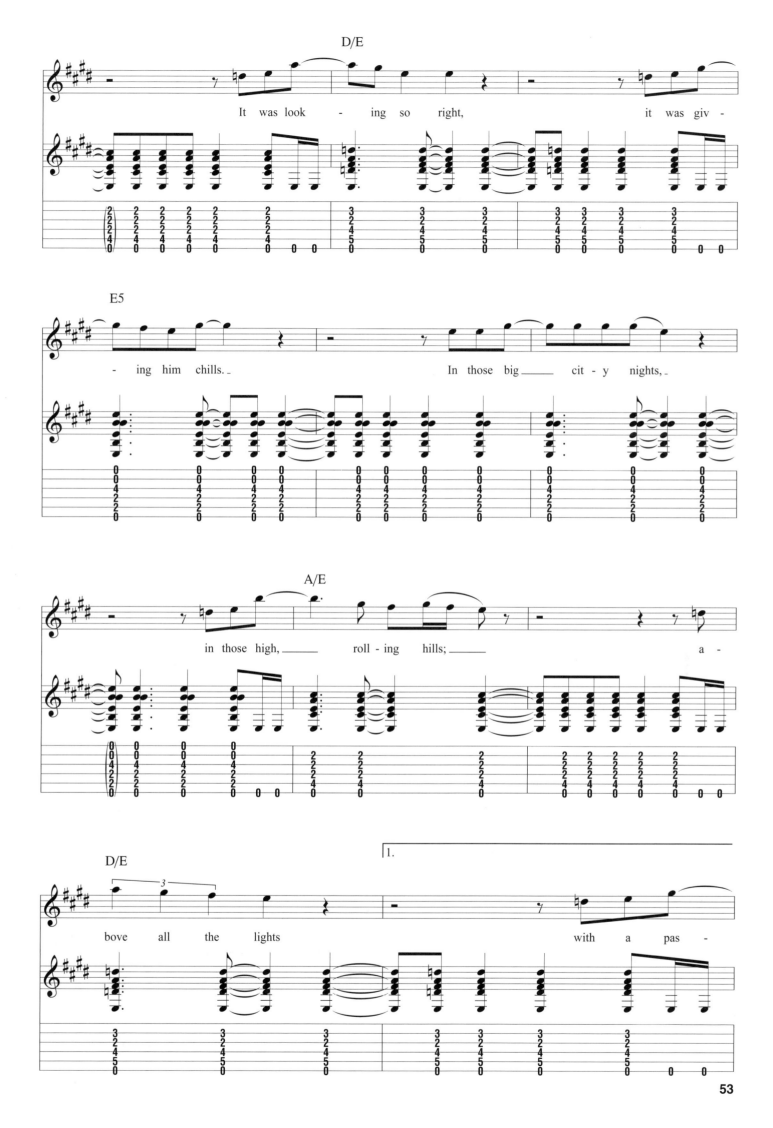

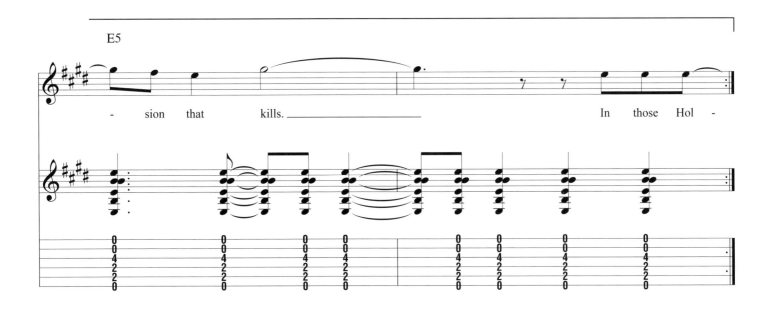

- sion that kills. _____ In those Hol -

2.

she had all _____ of the skills. _____

Outro
w/ Voc. ad lib., till fade

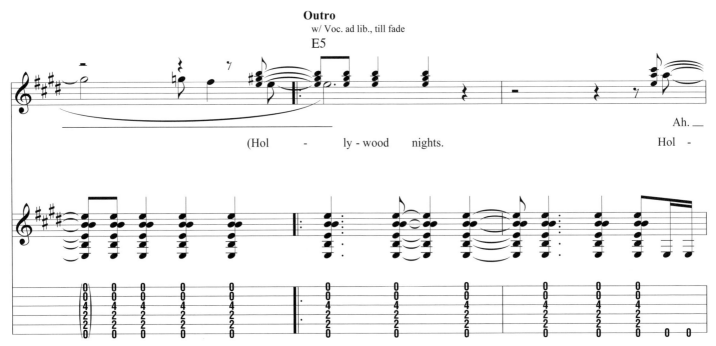

(Hol - ly - wood nights.

Ah. _____

Hol -

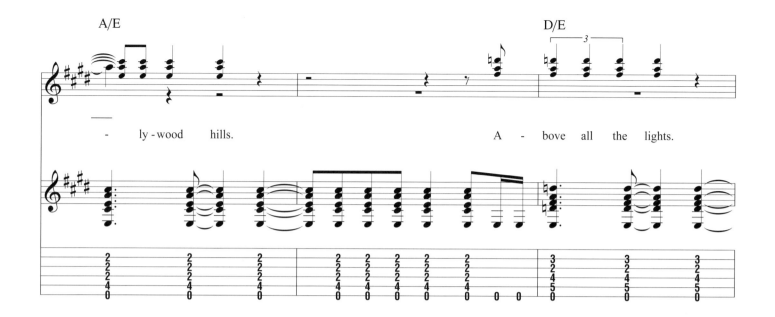

Play 4 times and fade

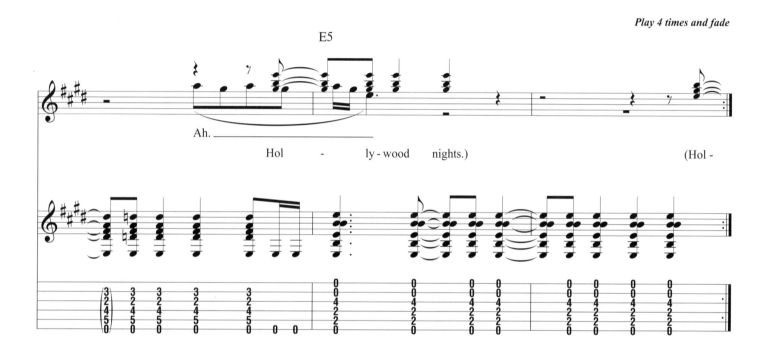

Additional Lyrics

Verse 3. He'd headed west 'cause he felt that a change would do him good.
See some old friends; good for the soul.
She had been born with a face that would let her get her way.
He saw that face and he lost all control.

Verse 4. Night after night and day after day, it went on and on.
Then came that morning he woke up alone.
He spent all night staring down at the lights of L.A.,
Wondering if he could ever go home.

Chorus In those Hollywood nights
In those Hollywood hills.
She was looking so right in her diamonds and frills.
All those big city lights
In those high, rolling hills;
Above all the lights,
She had all of the skills.

Like A Rock

Words and Music by Bob Seger

Capo I

Intro

Moderately slow ♩ = 80

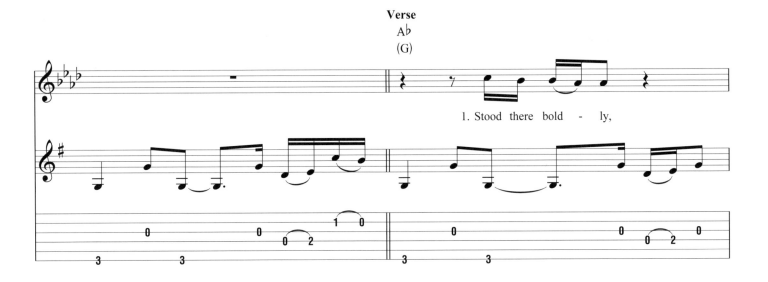

*Chord symbols in parentheses represent chord names respective to capoed guitar.
Symbols above reflect actual sounding chords. Capoed fret is "0" in tab.

Verse

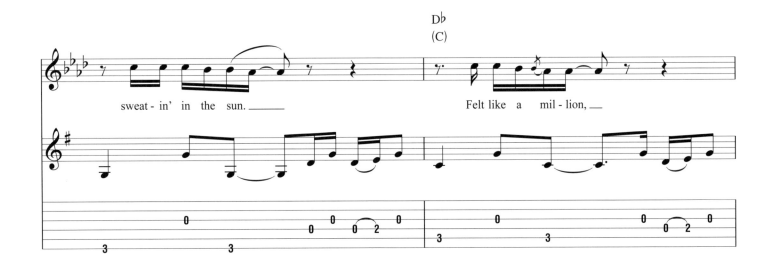

1. Stood there bold - ly,
sweat - in' in the sun. ___ Felt like a mil - lion, ___

proud, I stood tall,____ high ____ a-bove it all; _____ I

still _____ be - lieved _____ in my dreams. _

Guitar Solo

Hey!

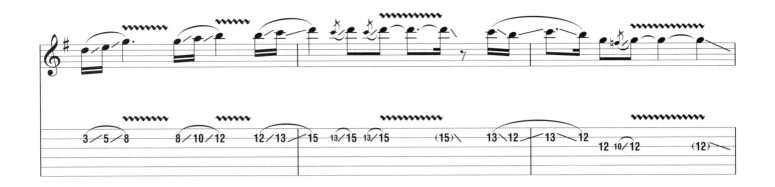

Db
(C)   Gbsus2
                                                           (Fsus2)

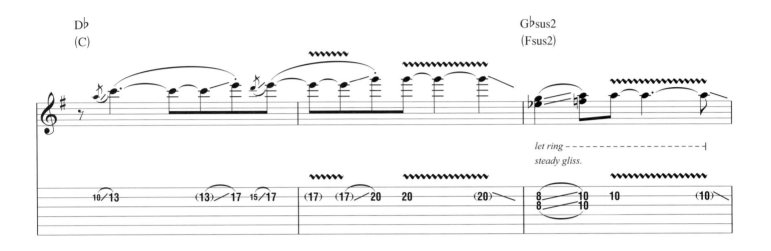

let ring ------------------------|
steady gliss.

Db   Ab
(C)   (G)

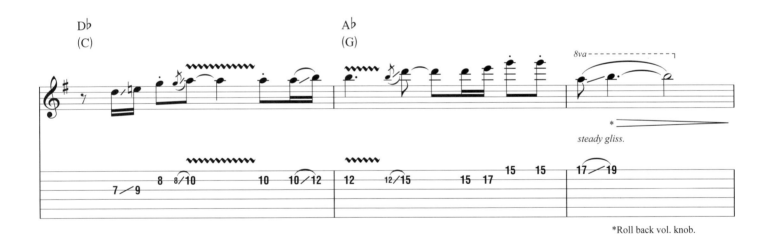

steady gliss.

*Roll back vol. knob.

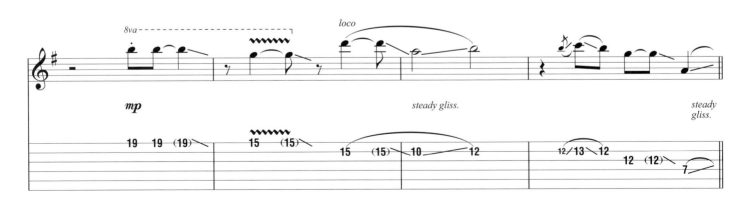

Outro-Guitar Solo

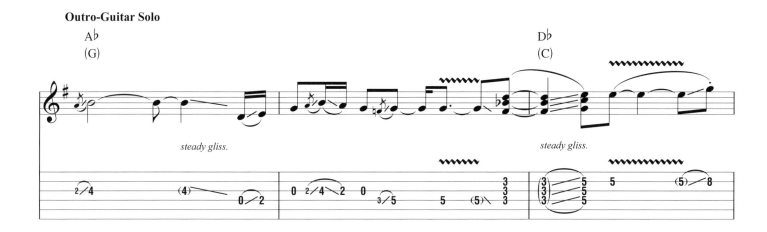

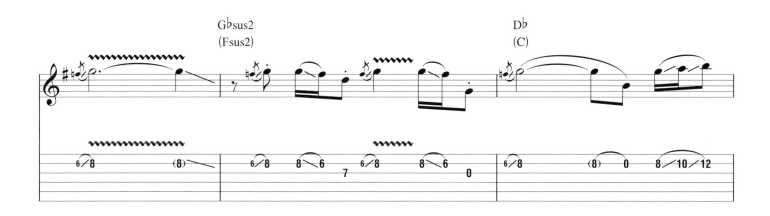

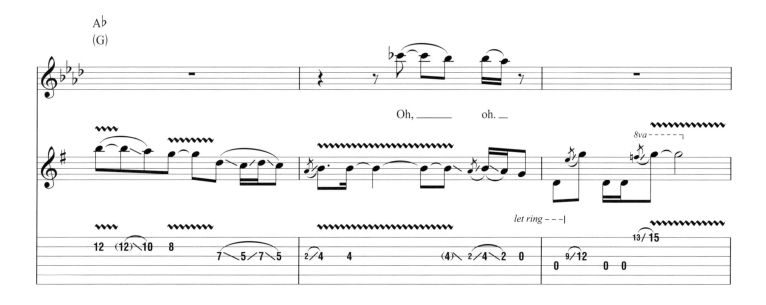

Oh, _____ oh. _

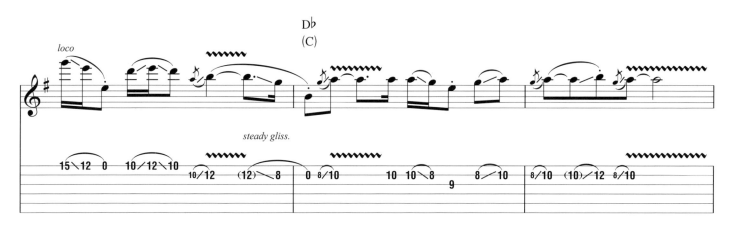

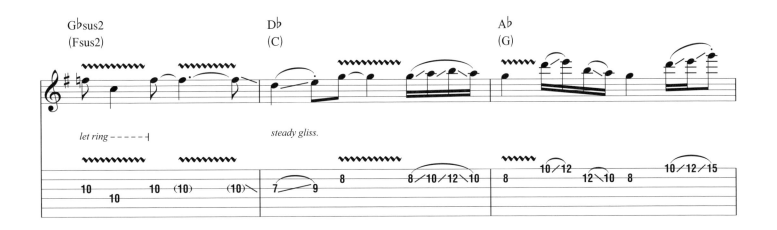

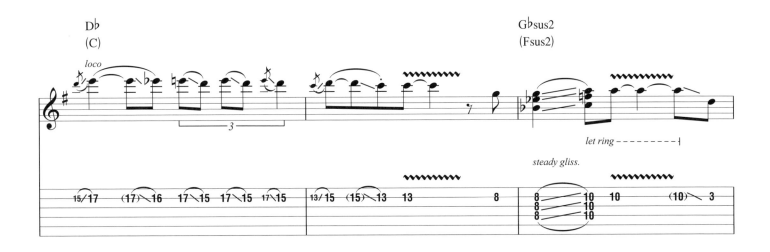

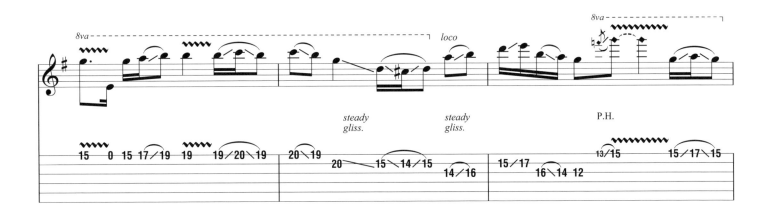

Free time

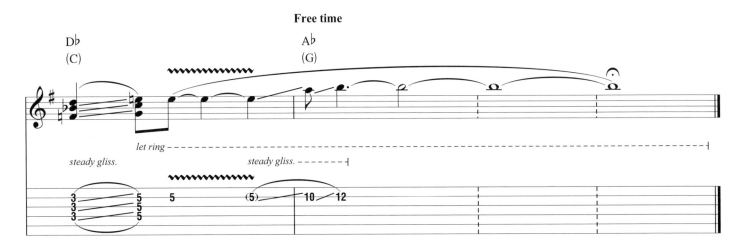

Mainstreet

Words and Music by Bob Seger

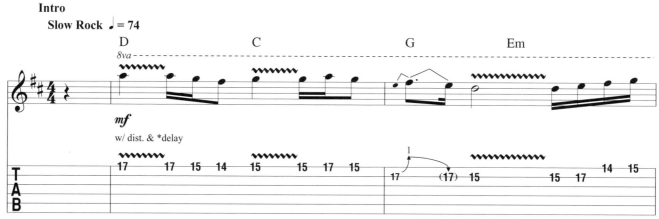

*Set for eighth-note regeneration with 1 repeat.

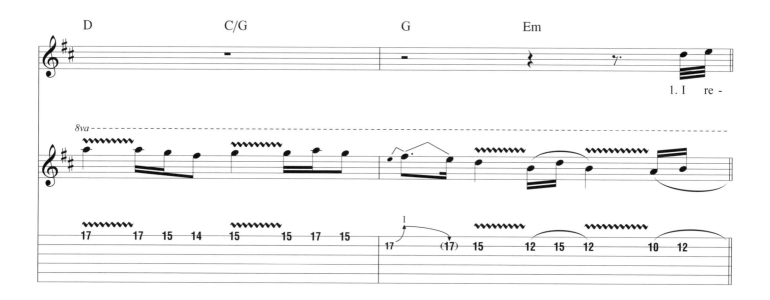

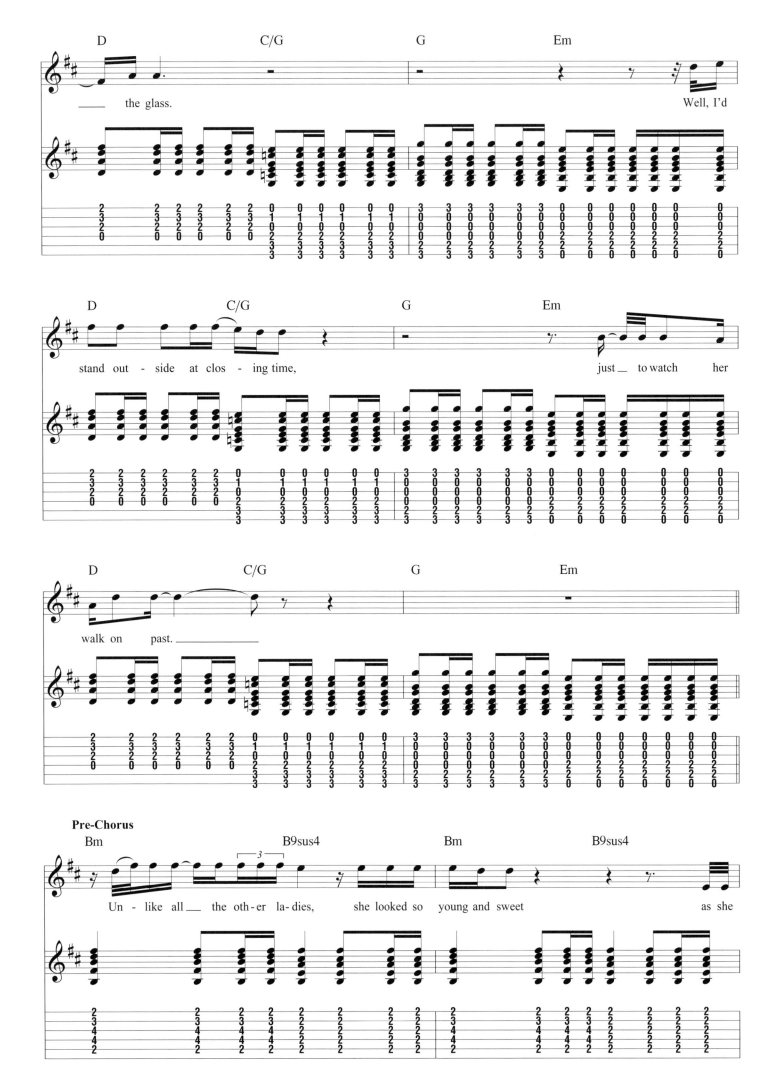

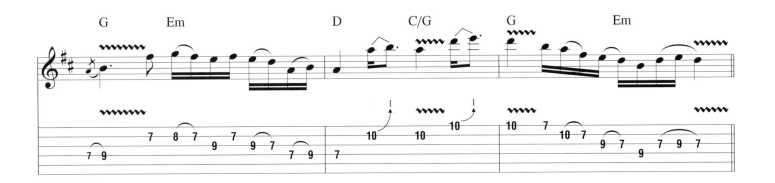

Pre-Chorus

Some-times e-ven now, when I'm feel-ing lone-ly and beat. _

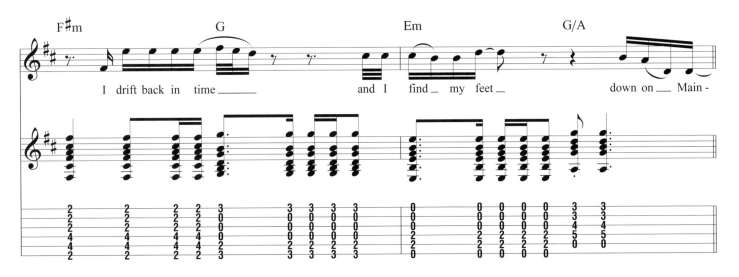

I drift back in time _____ and I find _ my feet _ down on _ Main-

Outro

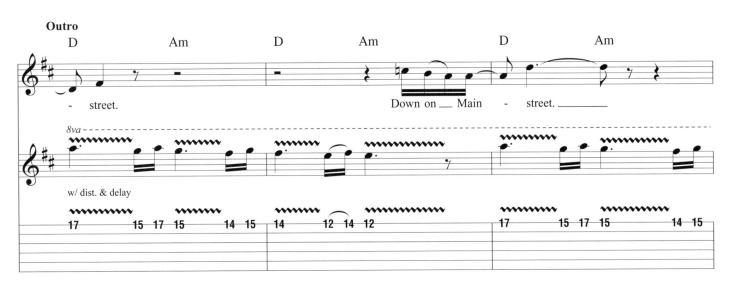

- street. Down on _ Main - street. _____

Night Moves

Words and Music by Bob Seger

Capo I

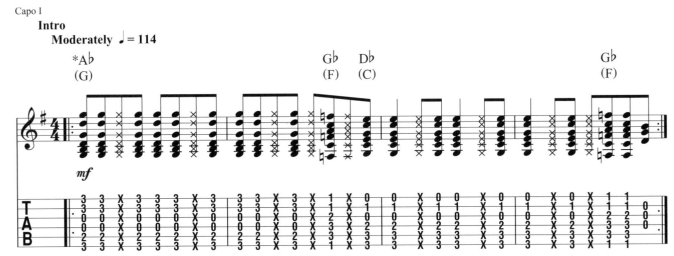

*Symbols in parentheses represent chord names respective to capoed guitar.
Symbols above reflect actual sounding chords.

Verse

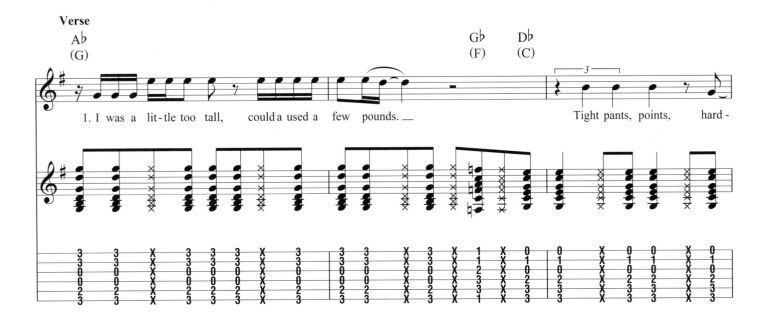

1. I was a lit-tle too tall, could a used a few pounds. Tight pants, points, hard-

-ly re-nown. She was a black-haired beau-ty with big, dark eyes,

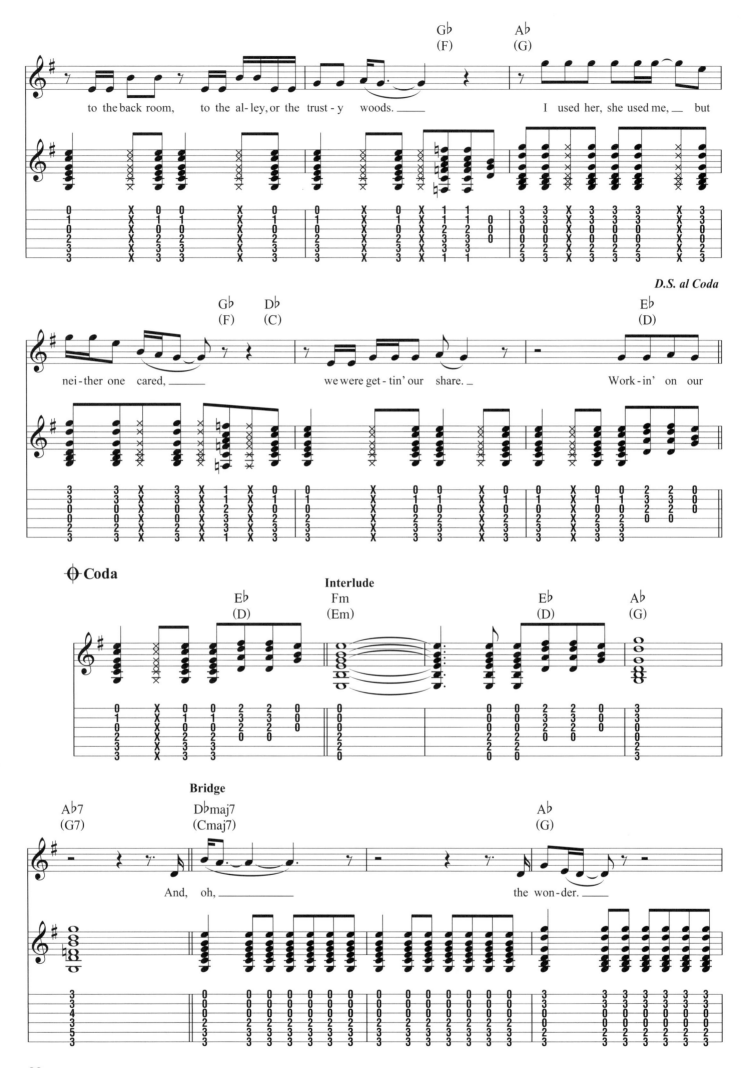

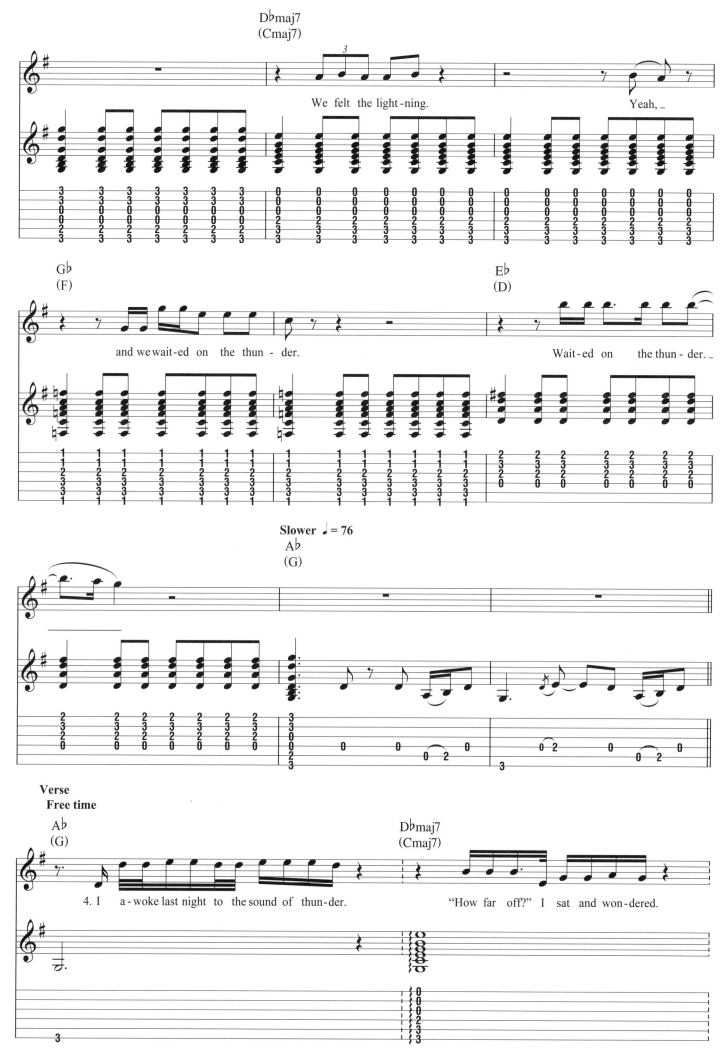

Start-ed hum-ming a song from nine-teen six-ty-two. Ain't it fun-ny how the night moves? When you just don't seem to have as much to lose. Strange how the night moves with au-tumn clos-ing in.

Moderately ♩ = 114

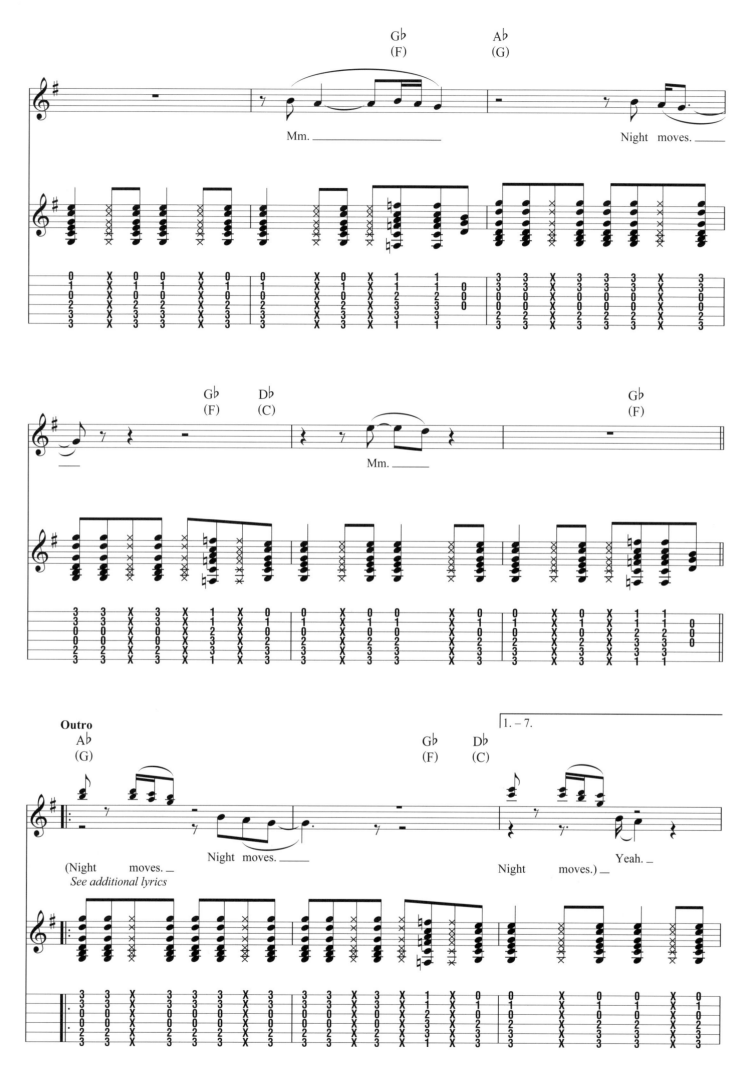

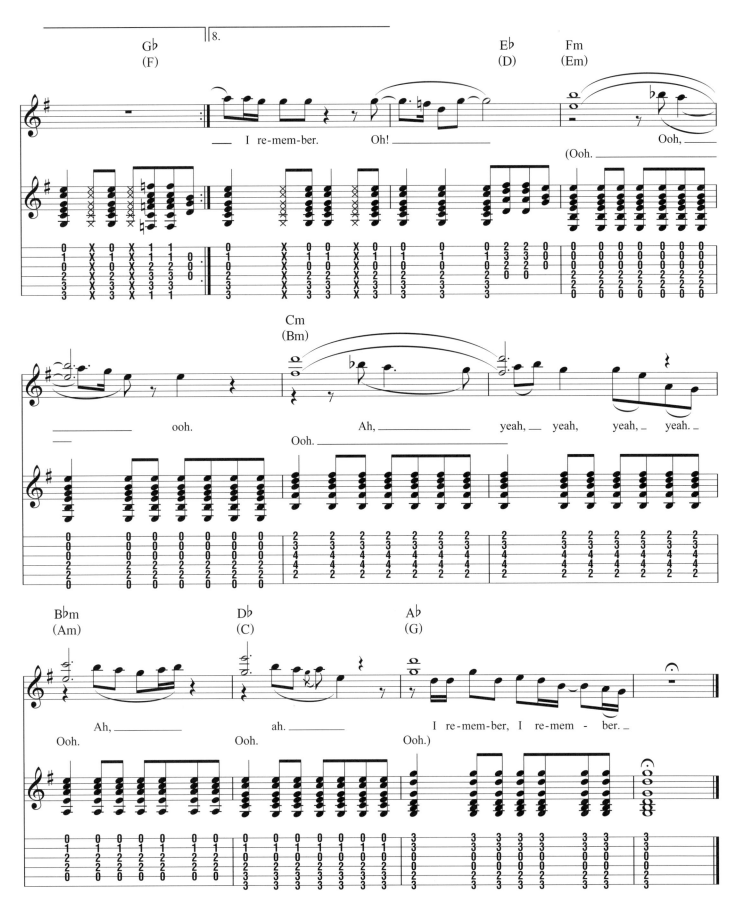

Additional Lyrics

Chorus Workin' on our night moves,
         Tryin' to lose the awkward teenage blues.
         Workin' on our night moves, mm,
         And it was summertime, mm,
         Sweet summertime, summertime.

Outro Moves, I sure remember the night moves.
     In the morning, I remember.
     Funny how you remember.
     I remember, I remember, I remember, I remember.
     Oh, oh, oh.
     Keep it workin', workin' and practicin'.
     Workin' and practicin' all of the night moves.
     Night moves. Oh.
     I remember, yeah, yeah, yeah, I remember.
     Ooh. I remember, Lord, I remember, Lord, I remember.

Rock And Roll Never Forgets

Words and Music by Bob Seger

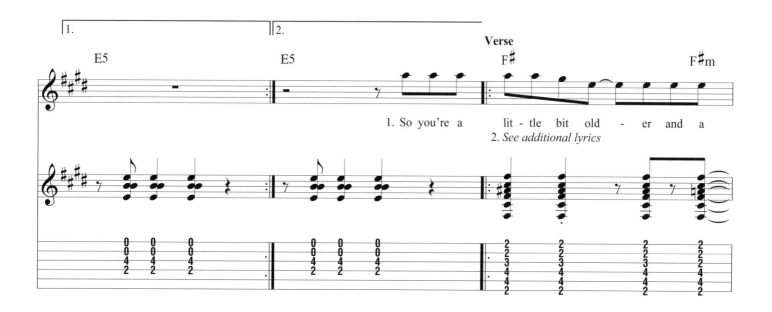

if you're in a fix.

Come back, baby, rock and roll nev-er for-gets.

2. You bet-ter

Oo, the

band's still play-ing it loud and lean. Lis-ten to the gui-tar play-er

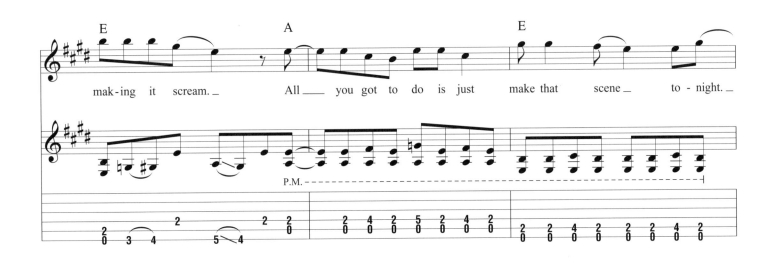

mak-ing it scream. ___ All ___ you got to do is just make that scene ___ to - night. ___

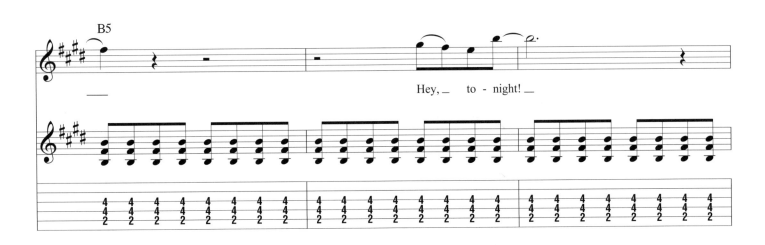

Hey, ___ to - night! ___

Guitar Solo

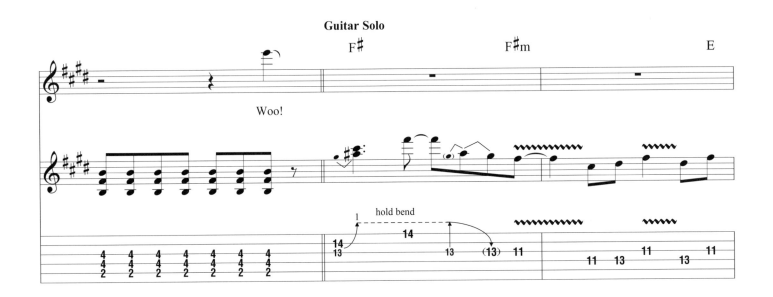

Woo!

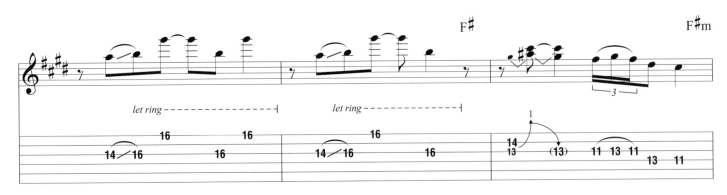

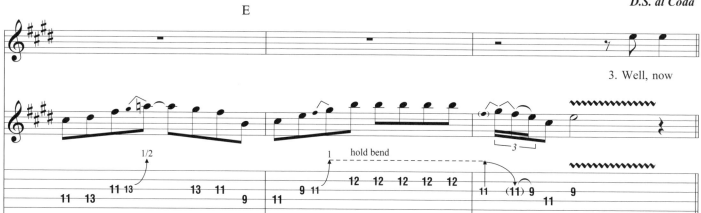

3. Well, now

Coda

Said you can come back, ba - by, rock __ 'n' roll nev - er for - gets. __

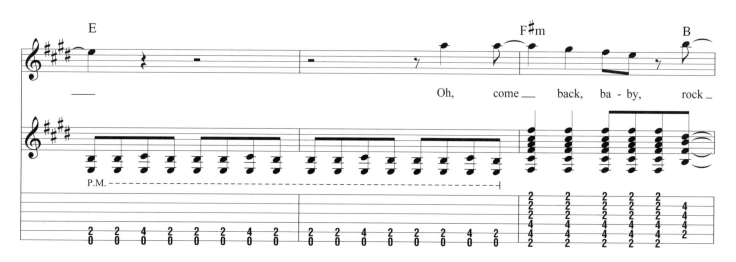

__ Oh, come __ back, ba - by, rock __

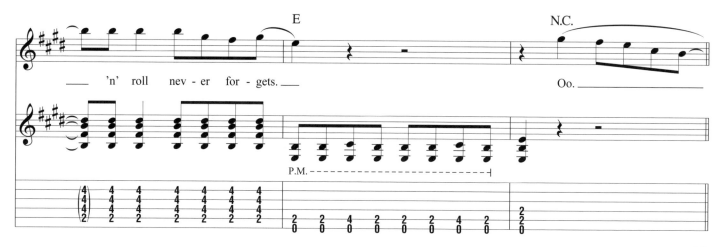

__ 'n' roll nev - er for - gets. __ Oo. _____

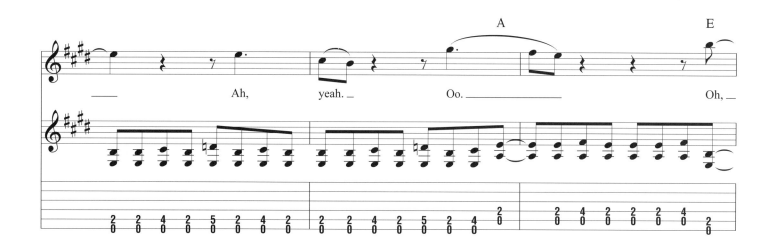

Outro-Guitar Solo

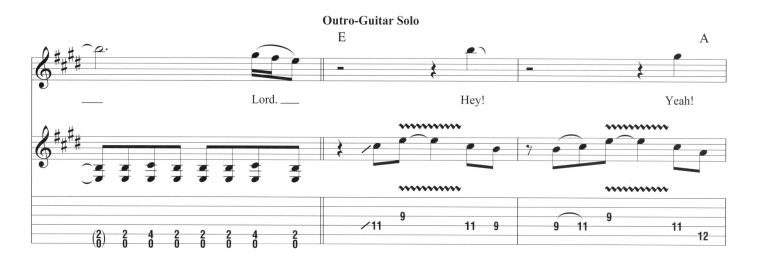

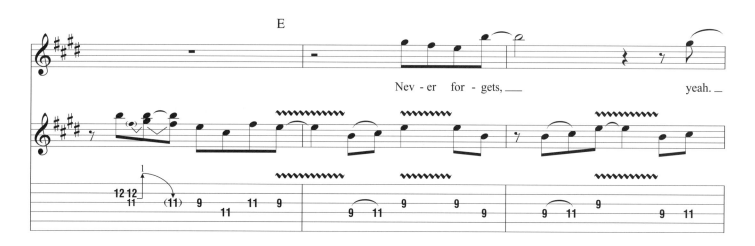

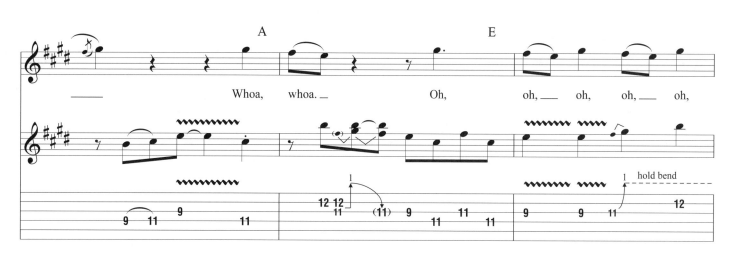

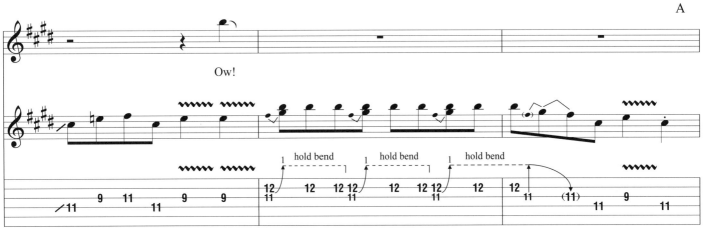

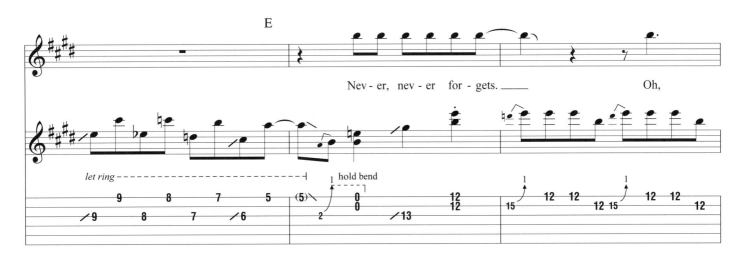

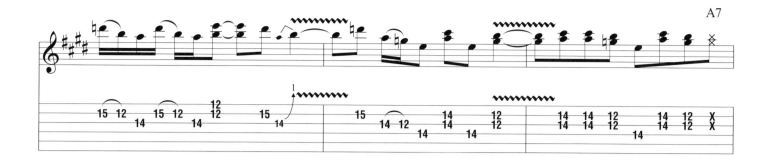

Begin fade

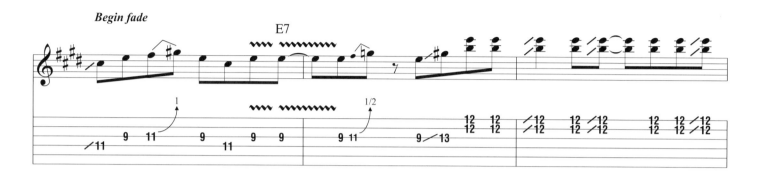

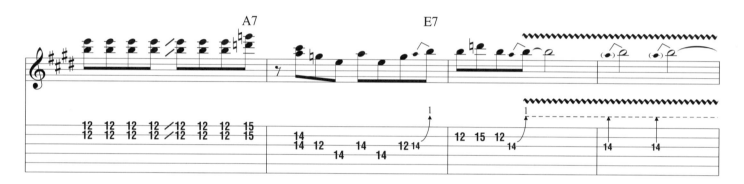

Fade out

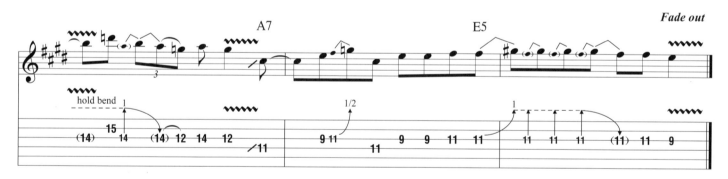

Additional Lyrics

Verse 2. You better get yourself a partner,
Go down to the concert or the local bar.
Check the local newspapers,
Chances are you won't have to go too far.

Chorus 2. Yeah, the rafters will be ringing 'cause the beat's so strong,
The crowd will be swaying and singing along.
And all you got to do is get in, into the mix.
If you need a fix.
You can come back, baby, rock and roll never forgets.

Chorus 3. Well, now sweet sixteen's turned thirty-one,
Feel a little tired, feeling under the gun.
Well, all of Chuck's children are out there, playing his licks.
Get into your kicks,
Then come back, baby, rock and roll never forgets.

Old Time Rock & Roll

Words and Music by George Jackson and Thomas E. Jones III

Tune down 1/2 step:
(low to high) E♭-A♭-D♭-G♭-B♭-E♭

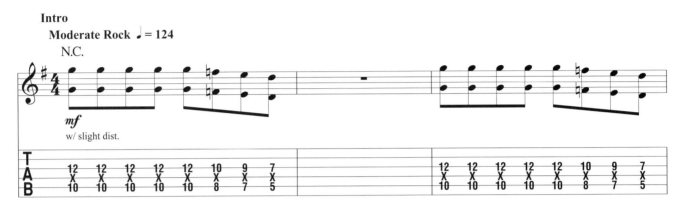

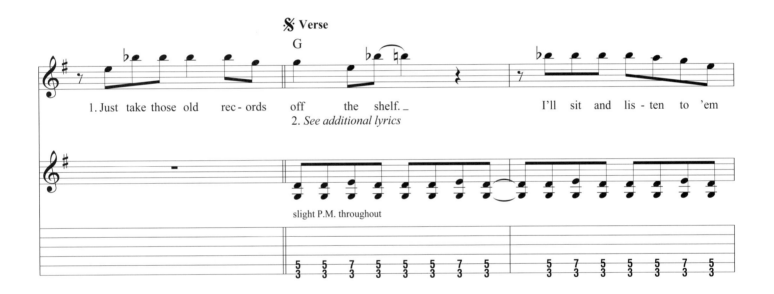

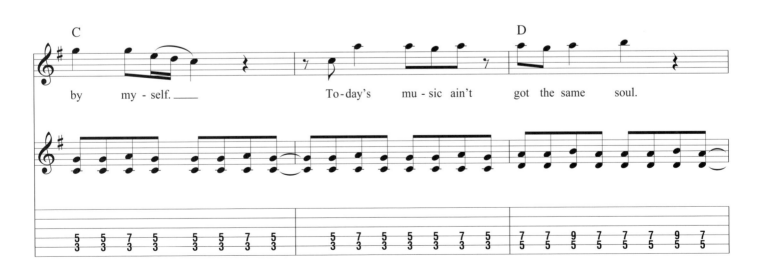

I like that old - time a rock and roll. ___ Don't try to take me to a

dis - co. ___ You'll nev - er e - ven get me out on the floor. ___

In ten min - utes, I'll be late for the door. I like that old - time a

G   𝄋 𝄋 **Chorus**
D   G

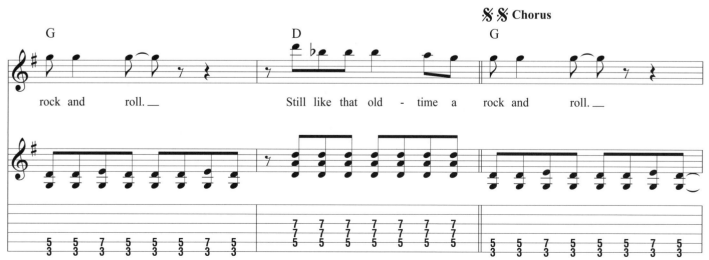

rock and roll. ___ Still like that old - time a rock and roll. ___

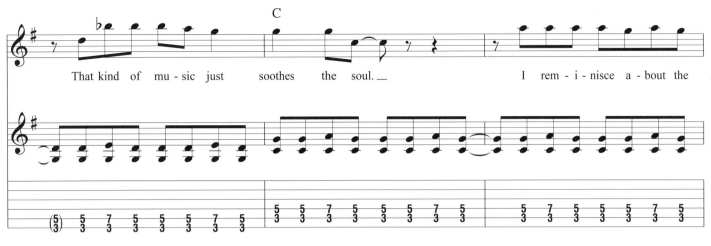

That kind of mu - sic just soothes the soul. ___ I rem - i - nisce a - bout the

To Coda 1
To Coda 2

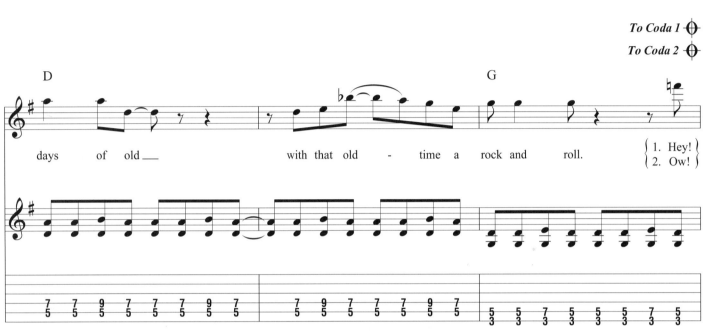

days of old ___ with that old - time a rock and roll.

{ 1. Hey! }
{ 2. Ow! }

Guitar Solo

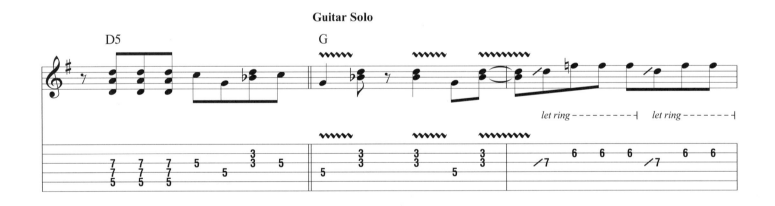

let ring *let ring*

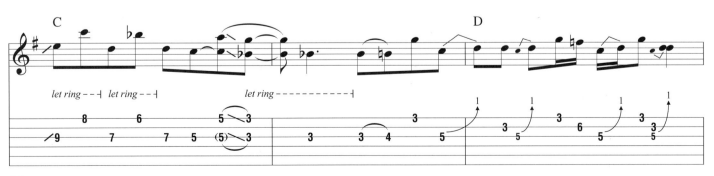

let ring *let ring* *let ring*

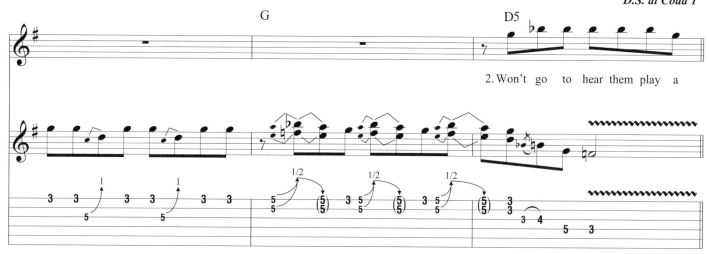

2. Won't go to hear them play a

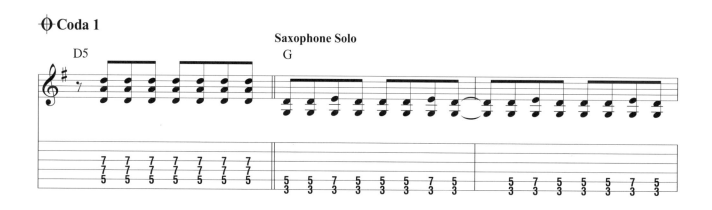

⊕ Coda 1

Saxophone Solo

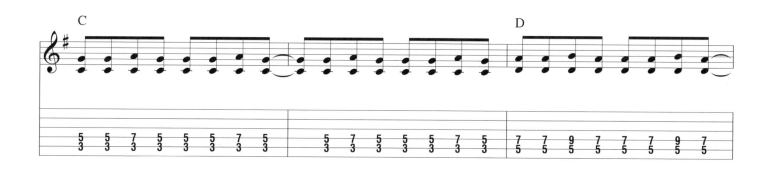

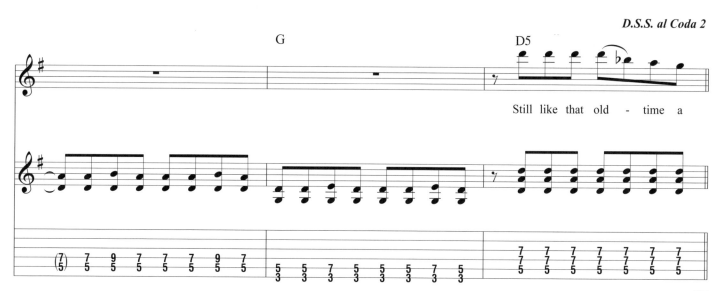

Still like that old - time a

Breakdown-Chorus

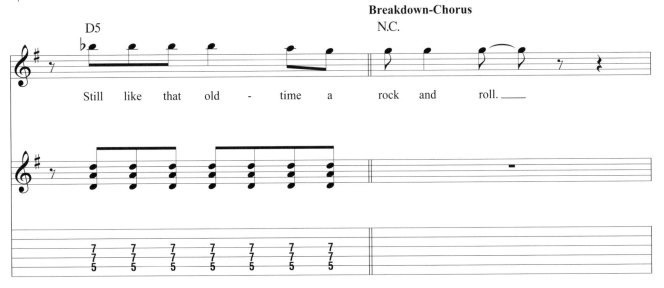

Still like that old - time a rock and roll.____

That kind of mu - sic just soothes the soul.

I rem - i - nisce a - bout the days of old ____

with that old - time a rock and roll. Hey! Still like that old - time a

Outro-Chorus

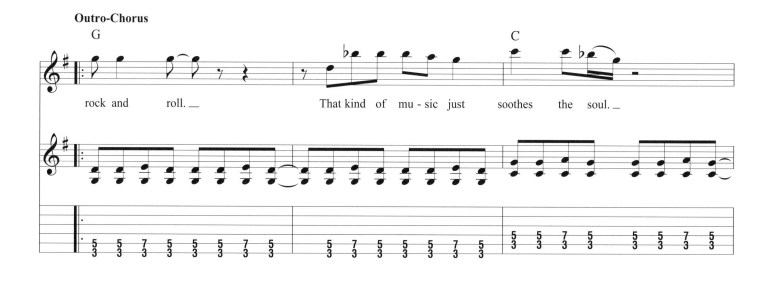

rock and roll. ___ That kind of mu - sic just soothes the soul. ___

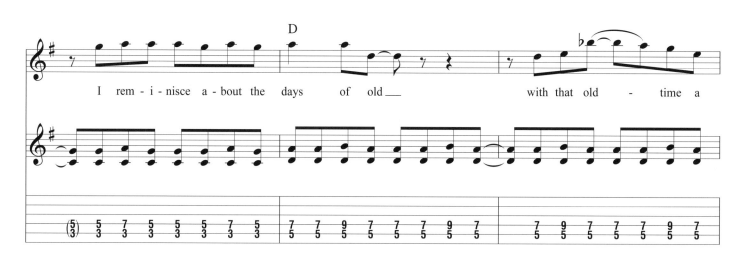

I rem - i - nisce a - bout the days of old ___ with that old - time a

Repeat and fade

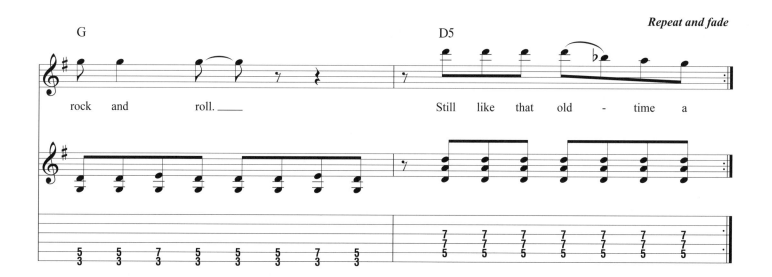

rock and roll. ___ Still like that old - time a

Additional Lyrics

2. Won't go to hear them play a tango.
   I'd rather hear some blues or funky old soul.
   There's only one sure way to get me to go:
   Start playing old time rock and roll.
   Call me a relic, call me what you will.
   Say I'm old-fashioned, say I'm over the hill.
   Today's music ain't got the same soul.
   I like that old time rock and roll.

Still The Same

Words and Music by Bob Seger

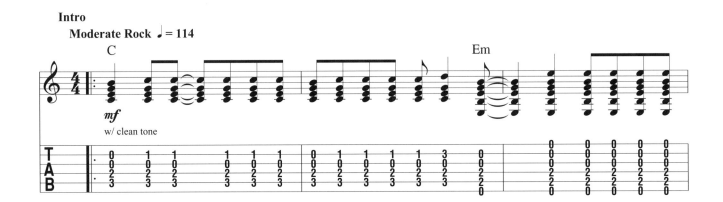

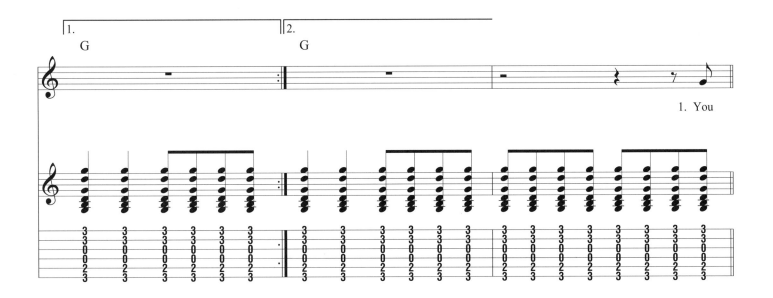

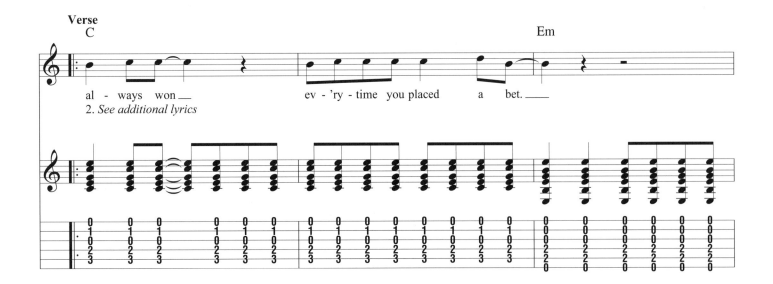

al - ways won ___ ev - 'ry - time you placed a bet. ___
2. *See additional lyrics*

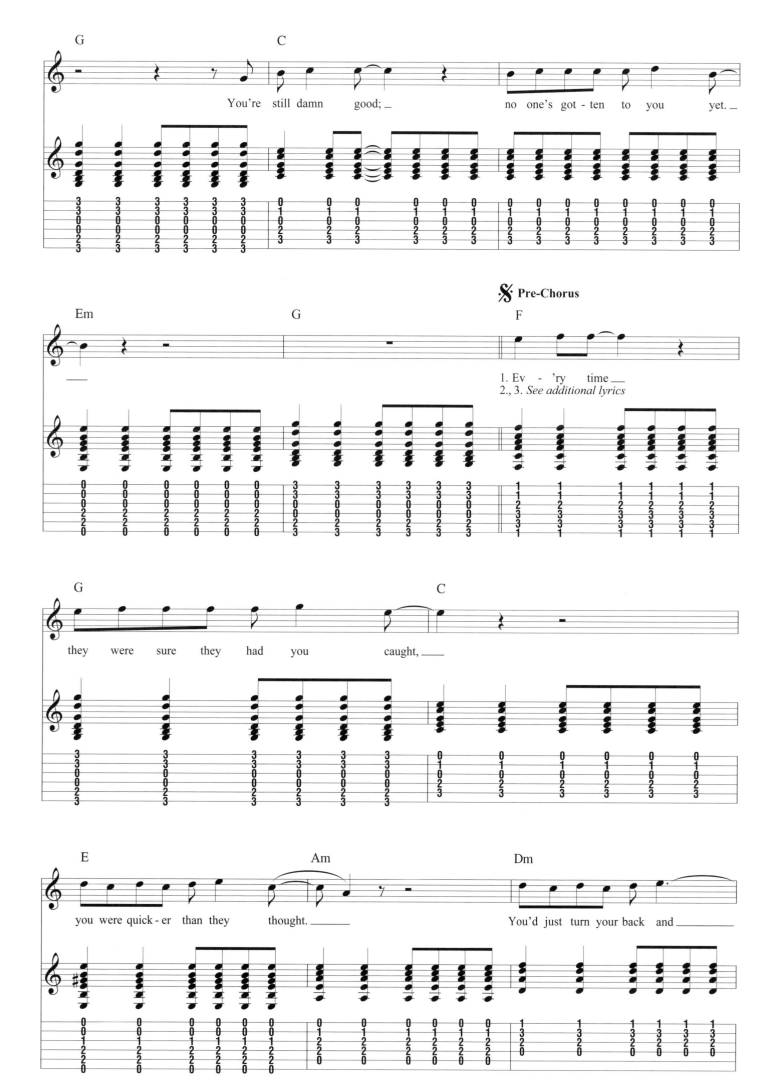

Pre-Chorus

1. Ev - 'ry time
2., 3. *See additional lyrics*

they were sure they had you caught,

you were quick-er than they thought.

You'd just turn your back and

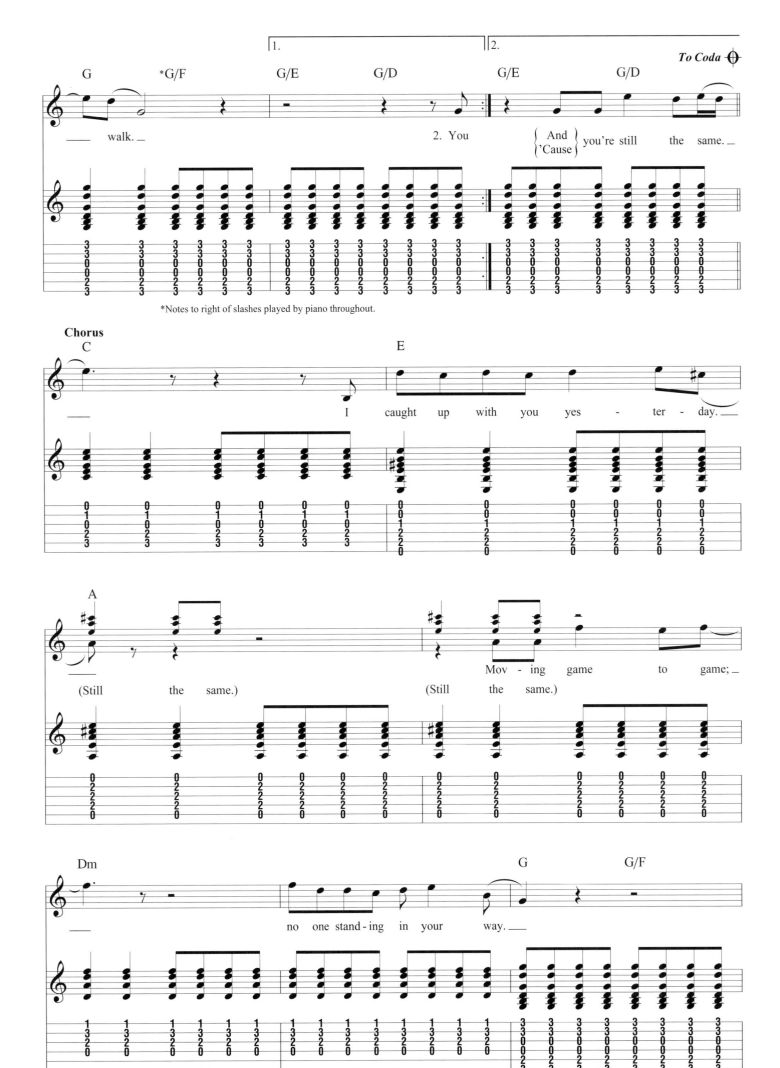

*Notes to right of slashes played by piano throughout.

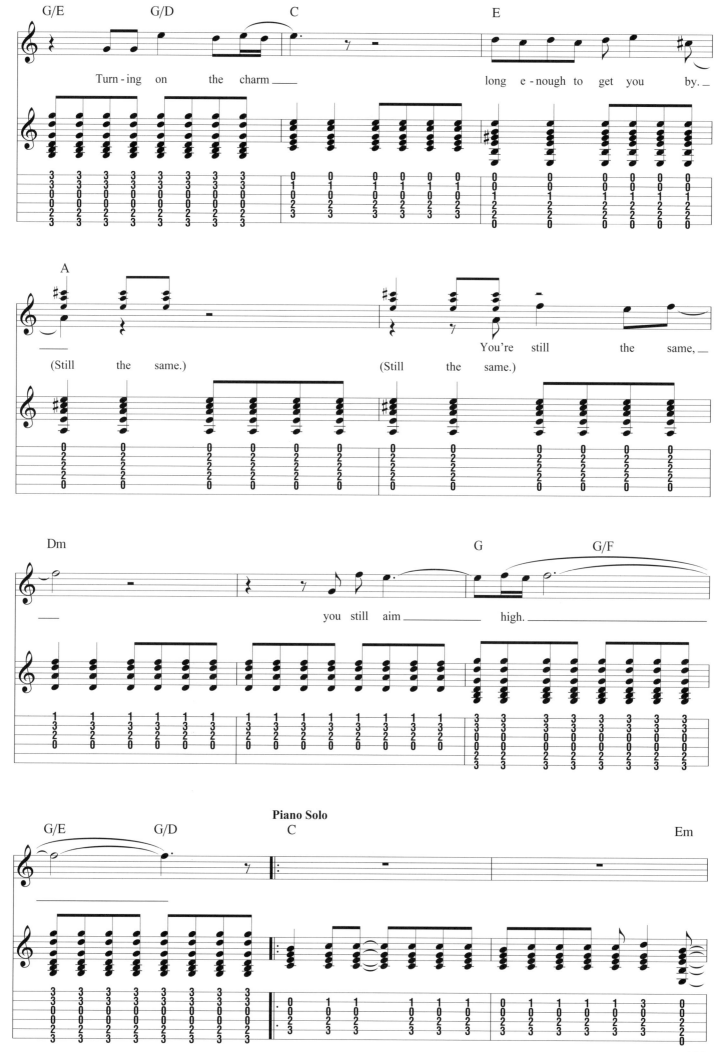

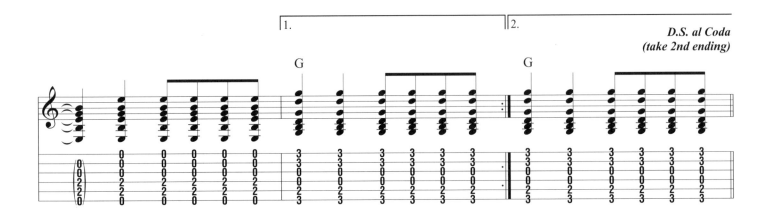

(Still the same, ____ ba-by, babe, you're still the same.) ____

Repeat and fade

You're still the same. ____

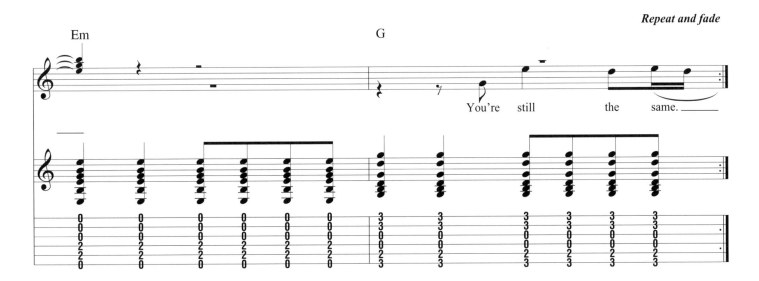

Additional Lyrics

Verse 2. You always said the cards would never do you wrong.
The trick, you said, was never play the game too long.

Pre-Chorus 2. A gambler's share;
The only risk that you would take.
The only loss you could forsake,
The only bluff you couldn't fake.

Pre-Chorus 3. There you stood; ev'rybody watched you play.
I just turned and walked away.
I had nothing left to say
'Cause you're still the same.

Sunspot Baby

Words and Music by Bob Seger

Intro

Moderately ♩ = 118

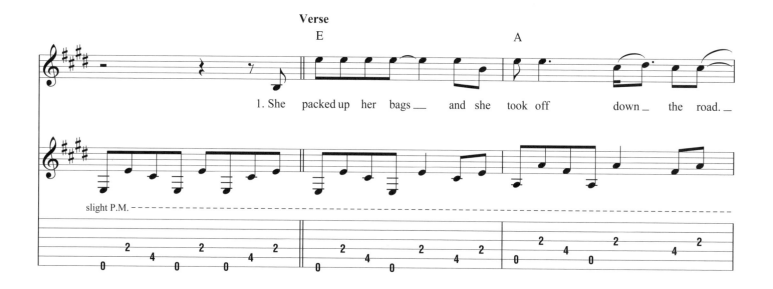

D.S. al Coda 1

Coda 1

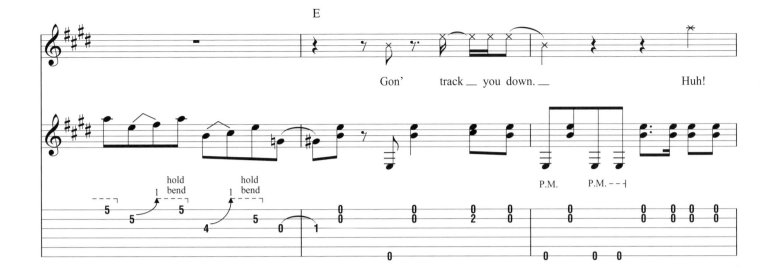

Gon'   track __ you down. __   Huh!

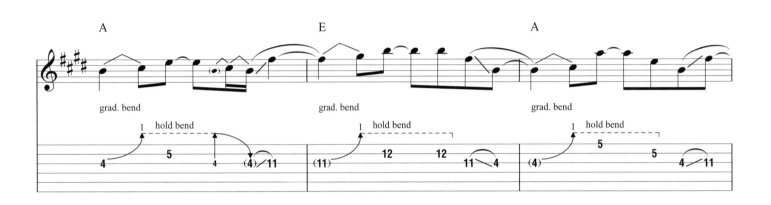

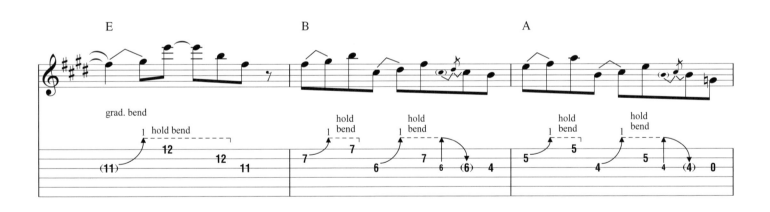

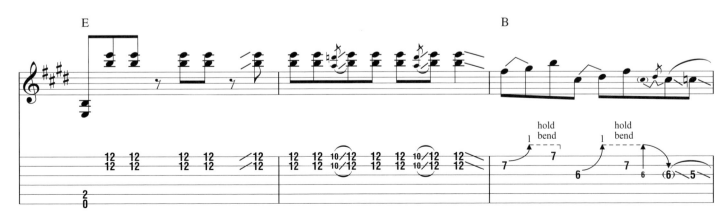

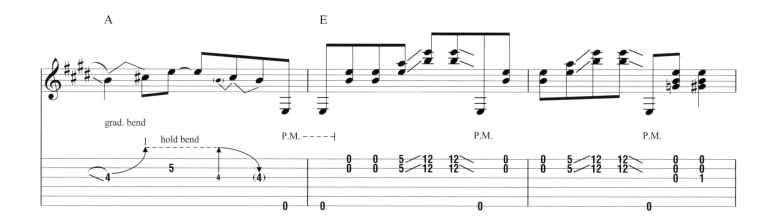

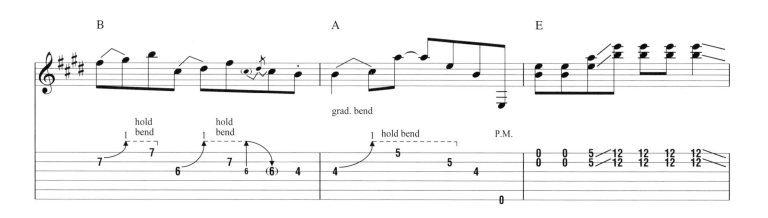

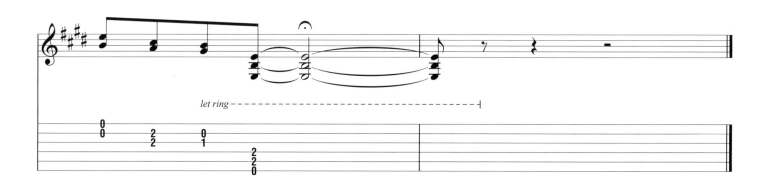

Additional Lyrics

3. But she packed up her bags; she took off down the road.
   She said she was going to visit sister Flo.
   Aw, she used my address and my name,
   And man, that was sure unkind.
   Sunspot Baby, I'm gonna catch up sometime.
   Sure had a real good time.

4. But she packed up her bags and she took off down the road.
   She left me here stranded with the bills she owed.
   She used my address and my name,
   And put my credit to shame.
   Sunspot Baby, sure had a real good time.
   Oh, Sunspot Baby. She sure had a real good time.
   Yeah, Sunspot Baby. I'm gonna catch up sometime. Sometime.

You'll Accomp'ny Me

Words and Music by Bob Seger

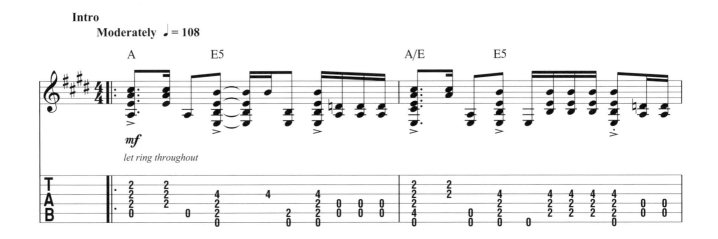

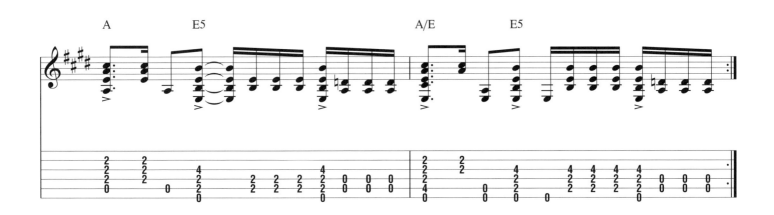

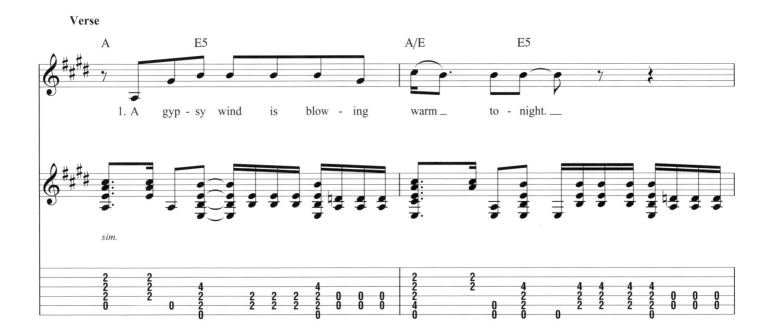

Someday, lady, you'll accompany me.

Someday, lady, you'll accompany me, yeah.

Interlude

Oo.

Verse

3. Some peo-ple say that love's a los-in' game.

You start with fire, but you lose the flame.

The ash-es smol-der, but the warmth's soon gone.

You end up cold and lone-ly on your own.

Chorus

Some-day, la-dy, you'll ac-com-p'ny me. ___
See additional lyrics

It's writ-ten down ___ some-where, it's got to be. ___

You're high a-bove ___ me fly-in' wild and free, ___ oh, _____

___ but some-day, la-dy, you'll ac-com-p'ny me. ___

Additional Lyrics

Chorus Someday, lady, you'll accomp'ny me,
Out where the rivers meet the sounding sea.
I feel it in my soul, it's meant to be.
Oh, someday, lady, you'll accomp'ny me.
You will accomp'ny me.

Turn The Page

Words and Music by Bob Seger

Intro
Moderately slow ♩ = 79

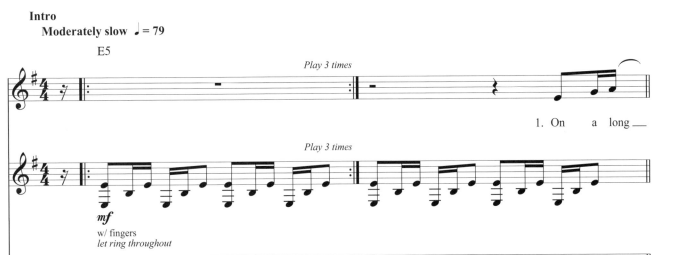

1. On a long

___ and lone - some high - way, ___ east of O - ma - ha, ___ you can
3. *See additional lyrics*

lis - ten to the en - gine ___ moan - in' out ___ his one - note song. You can

think a - bout __ the wom-an __ or the girl __ you knew __ the night __ be - fore. __

2nd time, substitute Fill 1

2. But your

Verse

thoughts will soon be wan - der - ing __ the way they al - ways do, __ when you're
4. *See additional lyrics*

Fill 1

ridin' six - teen hours __ and there's noth - in' much __ to do, __ and you don't __

__ feel much like rid - in', you just wish the trip __ was through. __

Mm. __ Say, here I am __

%. Chorus

on __ the road a - gain. __ There I am __

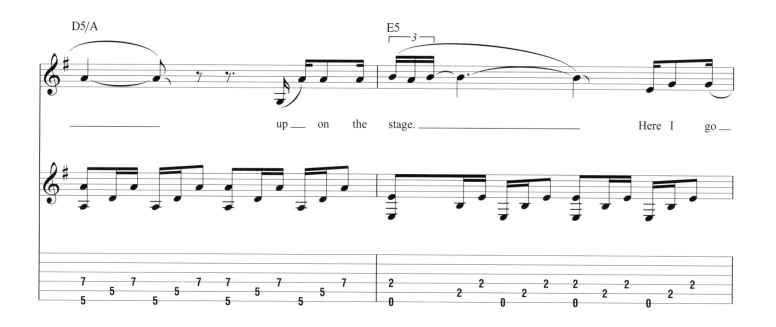

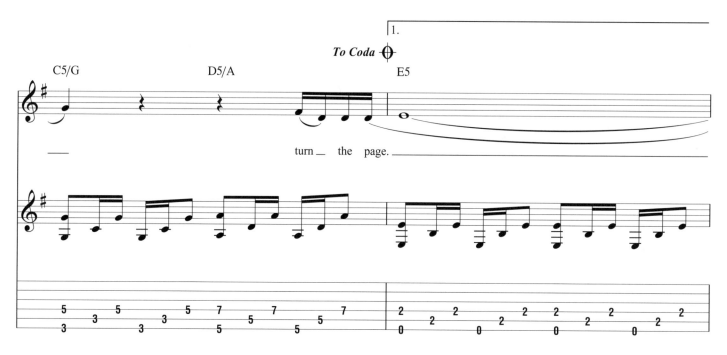

*Vol. knob swell

D.S. al Coda

Coda

Chorus

Ah, here I am, ___ ah, ___ on the

road __ a - gain. There I am, _____ up on _____

_____ the stage. ___ Here I go, _____ play- in' star __

___ a - gain. ___ There I go, _____

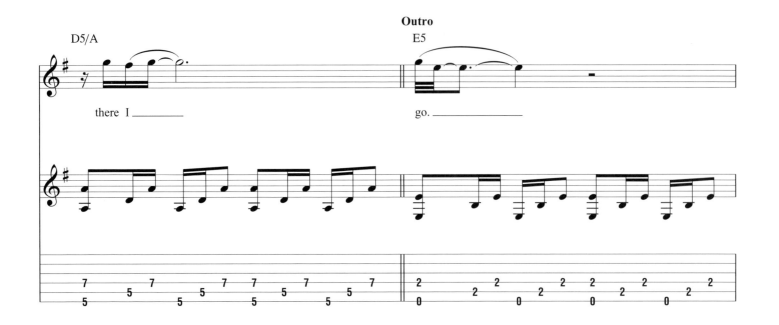

there I _____

go. _____

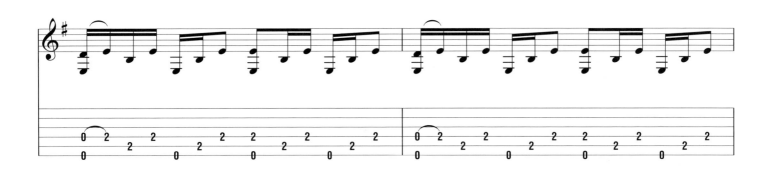

rit.

Oh.

rit.

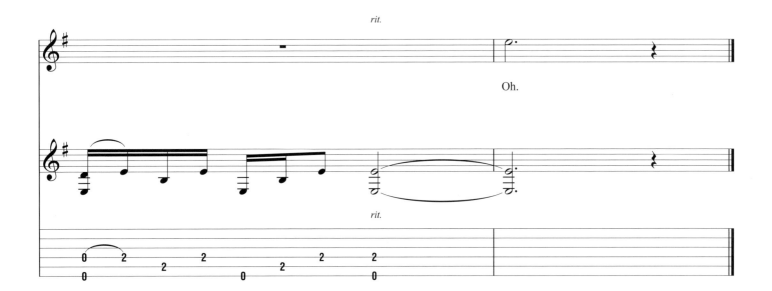

Additional Lyrics

3. Well, you walk into a restaurant, strung out from the road,
   And you feel the eyes upon you as you're shakin' off the cold.
   You pretend it doesn't bother you, but you just want to explode.

4. Most times you can't hear 'em talk, other times you can.
   All the same old clichés, "Is that a woman or a man?"
   And you always seem outnumbered; you don't dare make a stand.
   Uh, here I am...

DELUXE GUITAR PLAY-ALONG

The Deluxe Guitar Play-Along series will help you play songs faster than ever before! Accurate, easy-to-read guitar tab and professional, customizable audio for 15 songs. The interactive, online audio interface includes tempo/pitch control, looping, buttons to turn instruments on or off, and guitar tab with follow-along marker.

The price of each book includes access to audio tracks online using the unique code inside. The tracks can also be downloaded and played offline. Now including PLAYBACK+, a multi-functional audio player that allows you to slow down audio, change pitch, set loop points, and pan left or right – available exclusively from Hal Leonard.

AUDIO ACCESS INCLUDED 🔊

Each Book Includes Online Audio for Just $19.99 each!

1. TOP ROCK HITS
Basket Case • Black Hole Sun • Come As You Are • Do I Wanna Know? • Gold on the Ceiling • Heaven • How You Remind Me • Kryptonite • No One Knows • Plush • The Pretender • Seven Nation Army • Smooth • Under the Bridge • Yellow Ledbetter. 00244758

2. REALLY EASY SONGS
All the Small Things • Brain Stew • Californication • Free Fallin' • Helter Skelter • Hey Joe • Highway to Hell • Hurt (Quiet) • I Love Rock 'N Roll • Island in the Sun • Knockin' on Heaven's Door • La Bamba • Oh, Pretty Woman • Should I Stay or Should I Go • Smells Like Teen Spirit. 00244877

3. ACOUSTIC SONGS
All Apologies • Banana Pancakes • Crash Into Me • Good Riddance (Time of Your Life) • Hallelujah • Hey There Delilah • Ho Hey • I Will Wait • I'm Yours • Iris • More Than Words • No Such Thing • Photograph • What I Got • Wonderwall. 00244709

4. THE BEATLES
All My Loving • And I Love Her • Back in the U.S.S.R. • Don't Let Me Down • Get Back • A Hard Day's Night • Here Comes the Sun • I Will • In My Life • Let It Be • Michelle • Paperback Writer • Revolution • While My Guitar Gently Weeps • Yesterday. 00244968

5. BLUES STANDARDS
Baby, What You Want Me to Do • Crosscut Saw • Double Trouble • Every Day I Have the Blues • Going Down • I'm Tore Down • I'm Your Hoochie Coochie Man • If You Love Me Like You Say • Just Your Fool • Killing Floor • Let Me Love You Baby • Messin' with the Kid • Pride and Joy • (They Call It) Stormy Monday (Stormy Monday Blues) • Sweet Home Chicago. 00245090

6. RED HOT CHILI PEPPERS
The Adventures of Rain Dance Maggie • Breaking the Girl • Can't Stop • Dani California • Dark Necessities • Give It Away • My Friends • Otherside • Road Trippin' • Scar Tissue • Snow (Hey Oh) • Suck My Kiss • Tell Me Baby • Under the Bridge • The Zephyr Song. 00245089

7. CLASSIC ROCK
Baba O'Riley • Born to Be Wild • Comfortably Numb • Dream On • Fortunate Son • Heartbreaker • Hotel California • Jet Airliner • More Than a Feeling • Old Time Rock & Roll • Rhiannon • Runnin' Down a Dream • Start Me Up • Sultans of Swing • Sweet Home Alabama. 00248381

8. OZZY OSBOURNE
Bark at the Moon • Close My Eyes Forever • Crazy Train • Dreamer • Goodbye to Romance • I Don't Know • I Don't Wanna Stop • Mama, I'm Coming Home • Miracle Man • Mr. Crowley • No More Tears • Over the Mountain • Perry Mason • Rock 'N Roll Rebel • Shot in the Dark. 00248413

9. ED SHEERAN
The A Team • All of the Stars • Castle on the Hill • Don't • Drunk • Galway Girl • Give Me Love • How Would You Feel (Paean) • I See Fire • Lego House • Make It Rain • Perfect • Photograph • Shape of You • Thinking Out Loud. 00248439

10. CHRISTMAS SONGS
Blue Christmas • Christmas Time Is Here • Do You Hear What I Hear • Feliz Navidad • Have Yourself a Merry Little Christmas • I'll Be Home for Christmas • Let It Snow! Let It Snow! Let It Snow! • Little Saint Nick • Please Come Home for Christmas • Santa Baby • Santa Claus Is Comin' to Town • Sleigh Ride • Somewhere in My Memory • White Christmas • Winter Wonderland. 00278088

12. THREE-CHORD SONGS
Ain't No Sunshine • All Along the Watchtower • Bad Moon Rising • Beverly Hills • Can't You See • Evil Ways • I Still Haven't Found What I'm Looking For • The Joker • Just the Way You Are • Ring of Fire • Stir It Up • Twist and Shout • What I Got • What's Up • Wicked Game. 00278488

13. FOUR-CHORD SONGS
Chasing Cars • Cruise • Demons • Hand in My Pocket • Hey, Soul Sister • Hey Ya! • If I Had $1,000,000 • Riptide • Rude • Save Tonight • Steal My Girl • Steal My Kisses • 3 AM • Toes • Zombie. 00287263

18. KISS
Christine Sixteen • Cold Gin • Detroit Rock City • Deuce • Firehouse • God of Thunder • Heaven's on Fire • I Stole Your Love • I Was Made for Lovin' You • Lick It Up • Love Gun • Rock and Roll All Nite • Shock Me • Shout It Out Loud • Strutter. 00288989

19. CHRISTMAS CLASSICS
Angels We Have Heard on High • Away in a Manger • Deck the Hall • The First Noel • Go, Tell It on the Mountain • God Rest Ye Merry, Gentlemen • Hark! the Herald Angels Sing • It Came upon the Midnight Clear • Jingle Bells • Joy to the World • O Come, All Ye Faithful • O Holy Night • O Little Town of Bethlehem • Silent Night • We Three Kings of Orient Are. 00294776

21. NEIL YOUNG
Cinnamon Girl • Comes a Time • Cowgirl in the Sand • Down by the River • Harvest Moon • Heart of Gold • Helpless • Hey Hey, My My (Into the Black) • Like a Hurricane • The Needle and the Damage Done • Ohio • Old Man • Only Love Can Break Your Heart • Rockin' in the Free World • Southern Man. 00322911 ($24.99)

24. JIMI HENDRIX
Angel • Crosstown Traffic • Fire • Foxey Lady • Freedom • Hear My Train a Comin' • Izabella • Little Wing • Manic Depression • Purple Haze • Red House • Star Spangled Banner (Instrumental) • Stone Free • Voodoo Child (Slight Return) • The Wind Cries Mary. 00324610 ($22.99)

HAL•LEONARD®
www.halleonard.com

Prices, contents, and availability subject to change without notice.

HAL•LEONARD
GUITAR PLAY-ALONG

Complete song lists available online.

This series will help you play your favorite songs quickly and easily. Just follow the tab and listen to the audio to the hear how the guitar should sound, and then play along using the separate backing tracks. Audio files also include software to slow down the tempo without changing pitch. The melody and lyrics are included in the book so that you can sing or simply follow along.

INCLUDES TAB

Prices, contents, and availability subject to change without notice.

HAL•LEONARD®
www.halleonard.com

0820
173